Blaise Cendrars
Speaks...

Blaise Cendrars
Speaks..

Edited with an introduction by
Jim Christy

Translated by
David J. MacKinnon

Ekstasis Editions

The French edition of this book, *Cendrars vous parle*, was published by Editions Denoël in 1952.

Published in 2015 by:
Ekstasis Editions Canada Ltd.   Ekstasis Editions
Box 8474, Main Postal Outlet   Box 571
Victoria, BC V8W 3S1   Banff, AB T1L 1E3

LIBRARY AND ARCHIVES CANADA CATALOGUING IN PUBLICATION

Cendrars, Blaise, 1887-1961
[Blaise Cendrars vous parle. English]
    Blaise Cendrars speaks... / edited with an introduction by Jim Christy ; translated by David J. MacKinnon.

Translation of: Blaise Cendrars vous parle.
Includes bibliographical references.
Issued in print and electronic formats.
ISBN 978-1-77171-190-6 (paperback).--ISBN 978-1-77171-191-3 (ebook)

    1. Cendrars, Blaise, 1887-1961--Interviews. 2. Authors, Swiss--20th century--Interviews. I. Christy, Jim, 1945-, editor II. MacKinnon, David, 1953-, translator III. Title. IV. Title: Blaise Cendrars vous parle. English

PQ2605.E55Z8513 2016   841'.912   C2016-905242-7
                                                C2016-905243-5

Canada Council   Conseil des Arts
for the Arts   du Canada

Canada

Ekstasis Editions acknowledges financial support for the publication of *Cendrars Speaks* from the government of Canada through the Canada Book Fund and the Canada Council for the Arts, and from the Province of British Columbia through the Book Publishing Tax Credit. We acknowledge the financial support of the Government of Canada through the National Translation Program for Book Publishing, an initiative of the *Roadmap for Canada's Official Languages 2013-2018: Education, Immigration, Communities*, for our translation activities.

Printed and bound in Canada

Table of Contents

Who Is Blaise Cendrars?

"I am not of your race. I belong to a mongrel horde."
Blaise Cendrars

More than fifty years ago, Henry Miller, seeking an English-speaking audience for his literary hero, wrote that a small fortune awaited the publisher who dared bring out translations of the works of Blaise Cendrars. Ten years later, New Directions produced a selected writings; other translations followed but they never seemed to be the right ones, at least in regards Cendrars' prose which is not easily digested, and they were invariably the result of stodgy interpretations. It's like his keepers knew they had a thoroughbred but were afraid to turn him loose. The translators of his prose, with the exception of the estimable Nina Rootes, seemed intent on hobbling the wild beast; they never did Cendrars justice because they just didn't *get* him.

Whether there is a fortune in the current volume remains to be seen. If there was indeed justice in the world . . . .well, we know that old tune.

Now, at last, Cendrars has the perfect translator, a man after his own heart. A man who thinks like he does and who has lived some of the kinds of escapades Cendrars either lived or dreamed up. They are both linguists with a wide experience of work, travel, and study. If Blaise didn't go there, David has. Blaise had his right arm amputated; David was employed at a hospital where he carted amputated limbs to the incinerator; Blaise drove a tractor in Manitoba; David worked on an oil rig in Alberta. They both lived in China and in Africa. You get the point. MacKinnon has caught the rhythm of Cendrars' life and his writing. He *gets* him.

Like most native English speakers, MacKinnon came to Cendrars' work by way of Henry Miller, particularly a panegyric to the man included in *The Books In My Life*. I, however, approached from another angle, taking him head on, as it were. One day, long before I ever heard of Henry Miller from Brooklyn, a friend showed me a copy of that New Directions *Selected Writings* with its full, front cover photograph of the author. It had never occurred to me that writers might look like that. Cendrars resembled an old fight trainer in a French film from the Thirties or a guy just escaped from prison. In fact, he resembled Jean Gabin, only more so. The bags under his eyes had bags; his nose looked like a root vegetable, his eyes little eggs in a bird's nest of wrinkles (and in reality, bird's egg blue). People have written about his face; Charles Bukowski ever-jealous, ever-competitive, upon being shown the same book, produced a lousy poem about Blaise's work and his face, claiming the Frenchman's writing wasn't as good as the face and the man's mug was no match for his own. Be that as it may, Cendrars earned his face and, over a hundred years ago, invented modern poetry.

What kind of man was he? Cendrars was like your favourite uncle, your mother's brother who lived in a shack on a couple of acres down by the railway at the edge of town. Your father didn't care for him one bit. Uncle Blaise never asked if you liked school or if you had a girlfriend. There was an old Studebaker or maybe an Alfa Romeo out back, and Uncle Blaise let you drive it around the field and up and down the driveway before you turned twelve. Inside his place were books in six or seven languages, a Chagall on the wall hanging next to the Leger and postcards from Stravinsky. You never knew who was going to stop by. Therefore you met pinheads from Petawawa and professors from Pundachery; there was usually a gypsologist hanging around and that actress from Paris whom you considered an old babe but were confused by those long, shapely legs. – One thing I must add here that may seem like an aside, and is an aside, but is somehow appropriate because with Cendrars everything is an aside but each strikes at the heart of the matter and illustrates once again that nothing the man wrote is not exactly what it seems. For example, the title of his most famous prose work, the first ever novel about a serial killer: *Moravagine*. Some bright spark decided the title was a neologism meaning "death to the vagina." This has become the standard line but there is more to it than that. Although the eponymous protagonist slew scores of women, he left behind quite a trail of male corpses, as well. In all it was quite a total he ran up until fighting broke out in 1915 and stole his thunder. The "whole world began doing a Moravagine," as the author put it. Chaos and killing was his game. It has been noted that Cendrars was a gypsyologist and had traveled with the caravans. The basis of ROM culture, the key to its very existence is jiving the *gaujo*. In the Romani language moravagine means: "death toll", exactly.

Cendrars was a great talker but also a great listener, and always ready to lend a hand. *A* hand. At night Uncle Blaise would sit with you on the back porch and tell about the constellations and why fireflies light up the way they do. Also, he wasn't averse to slipping a dollop of rum into a young nephew's glass. If some of the stories he told seemed wildly improbable they were still interesting as hell, and he was never self-aggrandising like that old bore on the other side of town who called himself Papa. Now and again someone would fall by and verify the unlikely.

That's what Cendrars did. He verified the unlikely, presented the extravagant and the outrageous alongside the quotidian and the nitty gritty, and made the everyday marvelous. He enhanced life and revered it.

In these interviews, he ranges from Apollinaire's funeral to raising bees in 1910 with the help of a hunchback radical feminist. From getting drunk with Modigliani to cuddling with a girl while watching killer sharks near Montevideo. He talks about primitive artists in the Amazon and Jean Cocteau's wardrobe. He reveals the gypsy fortunes at the base of Brazil's early economy, remembers being on the set of Sarah Bernhardt's last acting job and provides a recipe for birds' nest soup as well as armadillo roasted in the shell. A ticket taker in the Metro gets as much space as Pablo Picasso because to his mind she is no less worthy.

His lust for adventure and knowledge, his passion for life are ever present in *Cendrars Speaks*. It's as if he knows just about everything but he wears his learning lightly. He imparts gleanings from the margins and the heart of the world out of the sheer joy of living and sharing.

The reader should be aware that odd things tend to happen when one becomes conscious of this one-armed man and a *flaneur* in what has been called Planet Cendrars, Two examples, a bookshop owner in Christchurch, New Zealand took me aside after I bought a copy of his poetry and, saying he had never met anyone who had heard of the writer, showed me the manifest of a ship that called at Bluff, New Zealand, and that listed Blaise Cendrars as a crew member. The odd thing about this is that the clique known as Cendrarsians will tell you he was never in that country.

In December, 1999, *The Georgia Straight* newspaper in Vancouver surveyed its regular contributors as to their nomination for "greatest writer of the Twentieth Century". I was the sole contributor not to put forth one of the usual suspects: Joyce, Hemingway, Gabriel Garcia Marquez. After I submitted the name Blaise Cendrars, the editor, Martin Dunphy, laughed, saying I must be making the guy up. He hadn't been able to find him in the standard reference books. But the notion of this obscure character assuming his place at the head of the pack, tickled his fancy, and Dunphy allowed me to do the essay. The result was that Blaise lovers came out of the woodwork, one being a 25 year female concert violinist and another, a man in his late- forties who lived under the Burrard Street Bridge, and who deposited a large manila envelope at the *Straight* office, containing a forty-five page stream-of-conscious improvisation on Uncle Blaise. I went to visit the fellow at his open air home and as we drank a cup of Lopsang soochong tea on his sterno-powered camp stove, he spoke of mathematics in Cendrars' work, particularly the angle of the propeller blades on Moravagine's "strut buster." He had been a professor of engineering at a two-year college in central British Columbia but insisted he was happier now.

Cendrars' influence is enormous. These days it is evident not only in writers like Ron Padgett and Jim Harrison but musicians and filmmakers such as Patti Smith and Jim Jarmusch.

The point of the above is to give you an idea of whom and what you're dealing with. He just wasn't like anybody else, much less like any other writer. Once you discover him, you're stuck with the guy. The reason one never bids farewell to Cendrars, leaves him by the roadside with the fallen literary heroes, is that he is just so damned interesting. As you are about to discover.

Jim Christy

Cendrars speaks…

As one of the twentieth century's most original writers, the poet vagabond Blaise Cendrars could conjure up words that confounded even his legendary cronies Apollinaire, Picasso, Braque, Chagall, the Delaunays, Reverdy and Modigliani. Cendrars was a beat poet fifty years ahead of Allen Ginsberg and Kerouac, a clown juggler who worked the circuses with Chaplin, a film-maker with Abel Gance, a collaborator with the Delaunays and Fernand Léger, a soldier with Curzio Malaparte, and a man who understood that media was about to converge in novel and revolutionary ways. He titled a series of his poems KODAK to codify his conception of each stanza as a snapshot of his travels worldwide. He once wrote a poem on 2 metre pages, placed each page end-to-end, in the identical height of the Eiffel Tower. His references were arcane or revolutionary – Mayakovsky, the Russian revolutionary artist who filled Red Square with his neon newspaper, an unknown aviator who carved out the words "Citroën" in smoke across the sky, and dotted the trema over the e while flying upside down, the levitating saints St Joseph of Cupertino and St Teresa of Avila. For a translator then, Blaise Cendrars presents a unique and very difficult challenge. Those who have attempted to bridge his world and ours have rendered tepid versions of his work. That is in no small part due to the fact that he is unclassifiable. Despite claiming to speak a dozen languages, he never wrote a word in English and the two English-speaking writers who knew him – Henry Miller and John Dos Passos – admired Cendrars from a distance and had no influence upon him. He not only disregarded the canons of literature; he made up his own rules. Depending on the day, he might deny that such a thing as literature even existed, as he did in his analysis of *Casanova's Memoirs*:

> "…notwithstanding the opinions of psychologists, moralists, historians, professional writers, there is no need whatsoever to have style, spelling, science, ideas, religion or even conviction of any sort to write an immortal book. Temperament and love of life are more than sufficient, and the mere inclination to amuse oneself by writing *true stories* without pretense and solely for one's own pleasure."

When feeling less prosaic, Cendrars might tear off a Gallic haiku, like

> "*The guillotine is the masterpiece of plastic art*"

or

> "*What's the use of documentation? I surrender to the impulses of memory.*"

Cendrars' testamentary wish was to have his ashes scattered over the Sargasso Sea. As a man, he was callous enough to refuse to lodge his own children, even during the worst phases of the Second World War, yet he could express heartfelt sympathy for the anonymous time-servers trudging out of the metro after a day of drudgery. He once punched out the pacifist Rilke with an upper cut from his remaining arm during a heated discussion on the war in the Closerie des Lilas. He was a jack of all trades, and mastered many of them, from soldier to watchmaker to beekeeper, assuming in turn the postures of Montmartre bohemian wild man cohorting with Modigliani, multi-media genius, deadbeat dad, fearless patriot, Brazilian buccaneer, polemist and unrivalled *raconteur*. He set his pen to every conceivable form of writing from epic poems to war reporting, ghost writing, ad copyist, and movie scriptwriter. In the end, as any "Cendrarsian" will tell you, you don't read Cendrars for character development or plot lines. It is because you, and others who have preceded you, have fallen under his spell.

Cendrars had an intense passion for modernity, but his enduring love was for the Middle Ages, that he liked to describe as "enormous and delicate", citing Verlaine. One suspects the influence of Albert Durer, and particularly his frame to visually divide a subject into grids, and the occasional physiological cruelty he displays is surely derived from his own hero and spiritual mentor, Rémy de Gourmont. In his poetry, you catch the ordinary mysticism of Hokusai's 36 views of Mount Fuji in woodblock print, the humorous philosophy and indifference of Chuang-Tzu and in his novels the absurd madness of Céline and Lewis Carroll. His descriptions of war evoke a Heironymus Bosch tryptich, as if he viewed his own experience through the retroscape of a man yet to be born.

"*There is no truth, only action*" says Cendrars, and that dictum provides another key to both his speech and his writing – it hinges upon cadence and tempo as much as the selection of words. And, yet, amidst the frenetic pace of his adventure and war novels, the contemplative man occasionally makes an appearance. Very few writers have the ability or inclination to "paint" a canvas in their writing; even fewer to bring musicality to poetry and prose. Cendrars attempted both, because as a master raconteur, and a former circus performer, timing, tempo and presentation were everything. Michel Manoll, who interviews Cendrars in the following pages, engages Cendrars immediately in a form of improvised creative sparring over the radio waves – prodding, provoking, cajoling, consoling, and his approach works. Cendrars could easily have clammed up like a shell, but instead he unleashes himself on the world, ad-libbing his way through the events, the inventions and the great characters of the twentieth century from Chaplin to Al Jennings, the great train robber, all of whom he knew, all of whom he instinctively understood because of his great sympathy for men who, like him, followed their own path.

Because the medium of radio – one feared by his contemporaries – suits him so well, Cendrars shines during the radio interviews in this volume. In a similar position, Breton insisted on writing down all his answers in advance. Cendrars on the other hand, insisted on improvising, and the interview becomes a jam session. Any rendering of the text – particularly in translation – has to take into account the theatricality of Cendrars' back-and-forth with the interviewer Manoll. He begins by talking of his father the inventor. Then he's onto his days as a ghost writer for Apollinaire. Suddenly, he confesses "I was a writing addict! Don't read, it's dangerous!" Or he refers to his thirty-six professions. His days as a whaler. Trapping armadillos. Cendrars derided Picasso as the son of a curator. He hated Breton the surrealist as a liar and a hustler.

Today, people increasingly resemble each other, not by virtue of their qualities, but by their lack of qualities. The individual is shunned, as if the reduced space on the planet has everybody thinking originality is a luxury for another time. Here is a man who stands apart, who fearlessly found his own path, and then, "held the posture" until the end of his time on the mortal coil.

Step into these pages then, and listen to the words he spoke – to their originality, their musicality, their humour, their occasional savagery, and more than anything, the love that this extraordinary man had for humanity in all its irregular forms and contours. Every word contained in this book was first spoken into a microphone in 1953, and only later transcribed, giving it an audio flavour, even though it appears in print form.

I

The Heist of the Mona Lisa

MANOLL: Was 1912 an important year in your life?

CENDRARS: Why do you ask?

MANOLL: Because Blaise Cendrars moved to Paris in 1912.

CENDRARS: In 1912, I wrote *Easter in New York*.

MANOLL: That was the year?

CENDRARS: You're right, Manoll. Yes, in 1912, I returned to Paris, because *Easter in New York* was published in Paris in 1912.

MANOLL: Still, it would be interesting to hear you tell how, and in what condition you found yourself at that time in New York.

CENDRARS: In 1912, during the Easter season, I was starving to death in New York, already for about ten months. I was starving to death because I didn't want to work and, when you don't want to work and you're not the son of a millionaire, you starve to death in the U.S.A like nowhere else, for the simple reason that you can never find a pal to break bread with, have a drink, borrow some money. It's not in their customs. From time to time, I accepted work, compelled and forced. But I never stayed more than eight days, and if I could get fired earlier and cash out my week, I did it, impatient to resume my reading down at the Central Library. That's how I became a tailor for women, for twenty-four hours on the recommendation of Madam Paquin, the creator of the pencil skirt, a friend of my godmother. For two or three sessions, I was pianist in a Bowery cinema. I worked for a whole week in the slaughterhouses, and couldn't bring myself to evacuate, *malheur*! I used to arrive at the Central Library at opening, eight o'clock am, and only left at 2 am, closing time. For the entire day I would dig into its treasures, ordering the most extraordinary books, and I wanted to read them all, all of them at once. I'd reserve hundreds at a time for the following day, and prior to leaving, I ordered more and more, hundreds and hundreds of others. When I left, the skyscrapers, in relief up against a polished steel-coloured, deformed New York night sky would start leaning off their vertical line, and you were convinced they were ready to fall on you if only you looked at them from the bottom to top, giving me vertigo. Meanwhile, another form of vertigo was making its way up from the depths of my entrails, this one caused by hunger, and I skulked for a long time in and around the taverns hoping to catch a scrap prior to returning to my faraway cell and go to sleep. The following morning, I was back at my workstation, my nose sniffing around the catalogues, ordering yet again new works for the day and digging my own hole inside the piles of books that I had reserved the previous day without managing to appease my fury to learn, to read, to know everything, which increased my fever more than the hunger that was devouring me. Hunger, thirst, the need for tobacco, ah the need for tobacco!...My misery was extreme and every day was marked by deepening misery, and there I was, unshaved, long hair, shoes worn down to the heel, trousers like a corkscrew, the jacket worn and wilted, button-less, no hat, no cravate in sight. I had sold my last cravate one day for one cent so I could purchase a can of the worst quality chaw in the world. I don't need to tell you that all the employees of the library knew who I was by then. One morning, as I was arriving at my usual place, one of the librarians motioned to me and said: "Come, sir, we have been informed about the type of books you order every day and the scope and the diversity of your readings. Come with me. We have prepared a small room for you, a small office. Your books are already there. We thought you would be more tranquil there for your work." And, sure enough, all my books were lined up in a row there. I had blank paper, carefully sharpened pencils, an assistant available to dig up any books I might need, dictionaries. That day, I looked inside all the drawers of the desk, thinking: "They are so kind, these officials of the Rockefeller library, that they didn't tell me out of consideration, but surely they must have hidden a chicken in the drawer..." No such luck. There was no cold chicken, no cigarettes. On the other hand, there was a typewriter. The time passed. Easter came. On Easter Sunday, the library was closed. Exhausted from turning in circles out in the street – well actually turning in squares, since all these American streets form blocks of buildings that are cut off at right angles – one evening, I entered a Presbyterian church where an oration was being given. *The Creation of Haydn*, announced the neon sign hanging from the bell tower. Inside the church, on one side, a scattered public and the other side, on a platform, young girls of the world, playing on mediaeval musical instruments and whose singing was divine. But a yokel of a bishop would interrupt the oratorio every five minutes to preach god knows what moral and to appeal to the good heart of the faithful. When the oratorio resumed, another yokel of a priest, just as boring as the previous one, entered the stall where I was sitting, to predicate gently to me on the merits of conversion, while sticking his paws down my trousers to extract a dollar or two for costs and shaking his leather purse under my nose. Poor me! I managed to squeeze my way out of there, and return on foot home, 96[th][2] Street West, absolutely disgusted and exhausted. It was around two or three a.m. I gnawed at a heel of hard bread and drank a large glass of water. I then lay down and immediately fell into a deep sleep. Some time later, I sprang up with a start and started to write and write. Then, I went back to sleep. I awoke a second time with a start. I wrote until daybreak and then went back to bed for good. At five pm, I woke up and reread what I'd done. I had spawned "Easter in New York".

MANOLL: The entire poem?

CENDRARS: As published. There were three erasures. End of story. All I wanted to do was get out of New York…

MANOLL: Where is this manuscript now?

CENDRARS: I don't know about the original, I probably sold it on a mashed potato day. But the publisher Pierre Seghers, a real friend to poets, who in 1948 had devoted a small volume to me in his collection *Poets of Today*, told me there was a copy of the manuscript that, if I'm not mistaken, is now in the hands of Paul Eluard.

MANOLL: He has it?

CENDRARS: Apparently. When I disembarked in Paris, I recall having left this copy at Guillaume Apollinaire's flat in Passy, *rue Gros*, just opposite the gas works. As to the name of the seller who Paul Eluard purchased the book from and date of sale, I couldn't answer that. I've never asked him, because I don't know Eluard. But Seghers, who had the copy in his hands, asked me for particulars on the layout of the manuscript, and what I told him, US paper format, written with my right hand, etc. seems to fit with what he had noted…[3]

MANOLL: How many years after you wrote it was the poem published?

CENDRARS: After I wrote it, I only wanted to leave New York, and within ten days, I had embarked to return to Paris. I paid five dollars, i.e. twenty-five francs. Imagine that in those days, you could return from New York to Paris for twenty-five francs! It's true that it was a cattle boat. As soon as I arrived in Paris, I published my poem.

MANOLL: Under what circumstances? You found a publisher?

CENDRARS: Are you kidding me? I found a printer, an anarchist who had a small clandestine press installed inside a piano box on the Buttes-Chaumont, *rue Botzris*, Villa des Boers. I worked with him to earn four sous on cost of publication. I took advantage of the opportunity to do my apprenticeship in typography. I did the typesetting for more than half the text. The chapbook was published with a cruel, demeaning sketch of me. It cost me around a hundred francs.

MANOLL: The run was…

CENDRARS: The run was around a hundred twenty-five copies. They were listed for twenty *ronds.** I didn't sell any.

MANOLL: Not a single one?

CENDRARS: No.

MANOLL: What happened to all these copies?

CENDRARS: But, where are your old papers, Manoll? I don't have a single copy.

MANOLL: Did it bring you any notoriety among poets?

CENDRARS: I was already known among poets because I used to mock them and interrupt their meetings at the Closerie des Lilas, the Café Fleurus and at the Procope. So, I didn't have to publish anything to become better known among poets. But, after the publication of *Easter in New York* in October 1912, I earned the enmity of the monks and the pontiffs who by the following year, when I published the Transsibérien, "the first simultaneous book" in June 1913, denounced me as an epigone and accused me of plagiarism. It wasn't just on to be a young authentic among all these decrepit legends emerging from the tail-end of symbolism, who all considered themselves as sacred bards. They all had beards. Couldn't help

---

* *sous*, or centimes

noticing when I laughed straight in their faces. I had built up my first stable of literary enemies. And *zut* for them if they've changed their minds since, but I doubt it.

MANOLL: For example, Guillaume Apollinaire?

CENDRARS: What are you talking about, Manoll? No, not Apollinaire.

MANOLL: Not Apollinaire? But you met him around that time in Robert Delaunay's studio.

CENDRARS: The truth is precisely the opposite! Don't listen to all these tall tales people tell these days to lead people to believe that they're well-informed just to stir up things. There's nothing to it. It's Delaunay who I met at Guillaume Apollinaire's flat.[4] Apollinaire was never an enemy. I never spoke ill of the man. I had known him for a long time. At the time, he was the sole poet who I actually visited. He was always kind to me and he gave me work that I could do to earn four sous. So don't listen to wagging tongues. He was influenced by me. It is said today, and it makes no difference to me; I sang the praises of the Eiffel Tower. He sang the eulogy to the Eiffel Tower. And quite a few others have sung its praises since. Neither they, nor Apollinaire nor I invented the Tower. It's Mr Eiffel himself who imagined it and who constructed it on a wager, and to amaze other engineers. Once, Apollinaire gave my name to a bearded gentleman named Henri-Martin-Barzun,[5] who published a modern aesthetic review, *Poésie et Drame*, and who had someone ask me for a poem on the Eiffel Tower. Of course, I gave it to him, this poem on the Eiffel Tower. He never published it. I ran across him one fine day at the counter of the post office on *rue Danton*. I asked for news of my poem. Barzun answered "Surely you don't imagine that I'll publish your poem on the Eiffel Tower when I have just completed a poem on the Eiffel Tower which is going appear in my next issue." "May God bless you!" I responded, "I hope that you aren't going to commit suicide by jumping off the Eiffel Tower..." A Polish tailor, inventor of a parachute vest, had just died while jumping from the highest platform into the void to test his new vest.

MANOLL: All the same, there is something extremely troubling, the change in poetic style of Apollinaire after your meeting.

CENDRARS: It was Jules Romains who was the first to observe this change of direction. Me, I couldn't care less.

MANOLL: You opened up broad horizons for Guillaume Apollinaire.

CENDRARS: It's not my business. It's the critics who are saying that. It's not my trade. I'm not really equipped for that type of thing. I sang odes to the Eiffel Tower when the desire took hold of me. I stuck this iron masterpiece into my poetry because I was horrified with the way poetry was being practiced. I was sick of it. Everybody knows that. The time of the Tower had come. It was the masthead of the T.S.F. It told the time to all the ships on the high seas. Why not to the poets?

MANOLL: It's not about the Eiffel Tower, it's…

CENDRARS: It's about the influence that I may have had on Guillaume Apollinaire. Robert Goffin[6] was one of the first to sound the siren, and god knows how many other people are wailing about it, as if it is a crime to be influenced by somebody.

MANOLL: But, no…

CENDRARS: Oh, yes. I sometimes get the impression when this alarm bell is rung that I'm not dealing with critics, students of poetry or historians but amateur police detectives who measure, distemper and take fingerprints.

MANOLL: So, let's get down to it. You claim that since the theft of the Mona Lisa, every poet had a police file down at headquarters.

CENDRARS: So? What's the big deal? We owe it all to Guillaume Apollinaire, who was accused of stealing *La Giocanda*.

MANOLL: So…

CENDRARS: When we knew, or at least everybody ended up knowing – right down to the last one of us – that the instigator of this whole disaster wasn't Apollinaire at all. It was D'Anunzio.

MANOLL: And D'Anunzio is?

CENDRARS: I've forgotten the name of the guy who actually pulled off the heist; it was an Italian, some guy named Perrugino, something like Perrugino. Picture the scene in the aftermath. Parisians were showing up in droves at the Louvre to stare into a blank square where the Mona Lisa had gone AWOL. It got so bad they had to erect barriers in the halls of the Louvre to corral the herd and file them in and out. I'm telling you, you'd have howled watching this circus. Even Dada didn't rankle the cuckolds as much as this caper. And the Louvre management was on eggshells, just completely panicking. The cops were tracking the lot of us.

MANOLL: How did they pull it off?

CENDRARS: Who knows? An Italian stole *La Gioconda*. He tore the canvas off the wall. He deflowered the virgin. He walked out of the Louvre with the painting under his arm. Like that. Nobody said anything. Even better! Nobody recognized the painting! True, there are a lot of copies of the Mona Lisa out there. Consider it. *La Gioconda* goes back home, returns to the fold, so to speak, and then there she is again, the runaway virgin back hanging in the same spot. If you want the facts, go ask Emmanuel Bourcier. He followed the case from start to finish, one end to the other, reporting for *l'Oeuvre*. He can give you the details of the adventure. He claims on his mother's neck that the canvas that was returned is a fake!

MANOLL: I don't get it. How does that get Apollinaire arrested?

CENDRARS: It's a long story. Apollinaire had a secretary, a Belgian. A bon *vivant* and a clown. A fake, but a fake who could get you laughing. Off the wall, just like the Mona Lisa. He was the one who cooked up the scheme. It all started with a bet for so-many bottles of champagne. The idea was to walk into the Louvre, select a Tanagra statuette, then choose a second, stick them under each arm and shake the hand of every security guard he met on his way out of the museum. The problem was it worked every time. Which of course meant he was storing the Tanagras in Apollinaire's flat, and that naturally left Guillaume with the problem. So, Apollinaire started handing out Tanagra statuettes to his friends. Here, happy birthday to you, have a Tanagra. Even Picasso got one. Apollinaire picks up the paper one morning. Big headline. **Sensational Theft** *of the Mona Lisa*! And poor Guillaume is petrified and for reason. As soon as the Louvre completes its inventory of collections – it will uncover another theft – the Tanagras. So, he decides to throw all his Tanagra statuettes into the Seine and be done with the whole business. Just as he cooks up that exit strategy, a loud knock on his door interrupts his thoughts. Bang, bang, bang! Picasso barges into his flat, panic-stricken, carrying a half dozen statuettes with him! "Here," he says, green with fear. "Take your bloody rubbish back… bring them back where they belong…this is going to end badly! Where the hell is that secretary of yours, anyways? He's put us in a fine fix!" But the secretary had slithered off into the reeds. Nowhere to be seen. Guillaume takes Picasso gently by the arm and says, "Pablo, maybe it's time for you to do the same. Clear out. Cover your own ass, Pablo, see what I care. Look, here's a hundred francs. Take the train to Marseilles and do your own disappearing act."

CENDRARS: The next day, on Picasso's advice, Apollinaire seals up the statuettes inside a wine-merchant's compartmentalized container so they're safe, and then delivers the Tanagras through Paris-Journal to the Louvre museum. He managed to retrieve most of them, although there could have been one or two still laying about in friends' flats. So, after a police investigation of about fifteen minutes, they already smell Polack blood and in a jiffy, Apollinaire is under lock and key. I still recall one of the headlines: *The Polack Kostrowitsky, operating under the alias Guillaume Apollinaire, head of a gang of international thieves specialised in pillaging museums, has been collared, convicted, and is now incarcerated in La Santé.* This is really what set into motion poor Guillaume's streak of bad luck. Go figure. Clearing his name took some doing. Anyways, this story has been told hundreds of times.

MANOLL: I'm very grateful to hear your version.

CENDRARS: The thief of the Tanagras embarked on a boat in Marseilles heading for Egypt, at that time under Turkish domination so as to avoid the danger of rendition, since France had no extradition treaty with Turkey. There was also an International Court of Justice in Cairo where any foreign national could seek seek refuge in the event he ran into problems with the authorities. Apollinaire's secretary had several aliases. I knew him under the name of Solway. When he arrived in Cairo, far from keeping a low profile, the rascal launched a tabloid, swaggered around for a time in society, and of course was identified and arrested. Then, in a gesture of bone-headed gallantry, instead of seeking the privileged protection of the Consulate of France, he appeared before a Turkish judge, arguing: "*Monsieur le Président*, I am a good Turk. The proof is in my seeking your protection and your high favour in order that I may enlist in the Turkish navy." At the time, Italy was at war with Turkey. The Italian torpedo boats were attempting to force an entry into the Dardanelles. A small Turkish torpedo boat succeeded in sinking one or two Italian torpedo boats, and possibly an Italian submarine, prior to being struck itself and sinking to the ocean floor. It would appear that a certain Solway was the commander of this miniscule torpedo boat. As far as I know, nobody's heard of him since.

MANOLL: I understand from what you have just recounted that you maintained an excellent relationship with Guillaume Apollinaire. Furthermore, following his death, you wrote a poem rendering homage to him, which was published…

CENDRARS: Yes, in the review *Sic*. But, already at that time, all sorts of rumours were circulating concerning him and me. André Derain, for example, was convinced that Blaise Cendrars was the last pseudonym of Apollinaire.

MANOLL: You have got to be kidding!

CENDRARS: Don't get it in your mind that I'm going to launch into some discussion concerning Apollinaire. Since he's now dead, poor chap, I'm not going to squabble with a corpse. If he were alive, we could brawl, it would even be enjoyable. But, not a dead man…

MANOLL: You saw him often. Would you call him a comrade?

CENDRARS: He was kind. He was charming. I worked for him as a ghost-writer, doing all the dirty work, just like he had done all the dirty work for Hanns Heinz Ewers,[7] this German man of letters, author of *Mandragore* and other horror tales, and with the advent of Nazism, he became Hitler's personal secretary.

MANOLL: Didn't you once go to Germany on his behalf?

CENDRARS: We went together for the opening of a Delaunay exhibition in Berlin. I think it was in 1913. Apollinaire spoke on the Eiffel Tower. I didn't get along with the director of the gallery, and I left without even giving my speech[8]...besides, I never did like Berlin.

MANOLL: What type of books did you do for Apollinaire?

CENDRARS: Since he had launched into erotica as a means to survive – it wasn't his Ingrès' violin* at all, as the saying goes – he really did it to survive – I prepared a number of erotic books for him. Some time later, he got into historical fiction – the series of *The End of Babylon, The Rome of the Borgias* etc. and it became a big joke. I think that I wrote the beginning of The End of Babylon, one, two, maybe three chapters, but I got sick of it pretty quickly and returned the whole package. I believe it was Maurice Raynal who took over, then René Dalize, and maybe even André Billy, you can check that with him. All the friends of Apollinaire collaborated in this series, writing a chapter or two.[9] Apollinaire had to submit the books to deadline, and if things didn't move forward...

MANOLL: And then, he shared the profits?

CENDRARS: No, oh not at all!

MANOLL: So, it was done out of kindness?

CENDRARS: No, like I said, it was all a bit of a lark. Apollinaire would front for a good dinner. We all had a good laugh.

MANOLL: At this time, you lived in the *rue de Savoie*. Was it prior to this or later that you were a beekeeper nearby Meaux?

CENDRARS: Oh, long before, of course, in 1907...

MANOLL: That's amusing, because you have said that you were earning 8000 francs per annum on honey.

---

* an activity undertaken outside of one's profession out of passion, rather than profit.

CENDRARS: I was a millionaire!

MANOLL: It seems a bit incredible.

CENDRARS: I was making 8000 francs on the honey and 30 000 francs on pears.

MANOLL: Net?

CENDRARS: Net. I was a millionaire!

MANOLL: You've always found a way to earn your living. During the occupation, you lived in large part on the proceeds of herbs, plants that you were growing in your garden in Aix-en-Provence.

CENDRARS: Medicinal herbs and plants.

MANOLL: You have an interest in bees?

CENDRARS: I became interested in bees because it generated a lot of revenues, I wasn't interested in the manner of Maeterlinck, supposedly to study the habits of bees and to draw absurd moral conclusions applicable to man. You thus meet thousands of people throughout the world who have this passion for the life of bees or ants and who explain their pastime as a study of social organisation. They're dead wrong in my opinion, because insects have neither morals nor any sense of justice. I made honey because it was easy work and it generated cash-flow. You just have to have a good client base. The other stuff didn't interest me. A capitalist in the neighbourhood paid one sou per day to a good old chap to take care of his bees. He was an invalid from the war of 70. He had a wooden leg. I offered two sous per day, plus a liter of red, plus a pack of tobacco, and the old man set up quarters at my place. He was happy. I gave him a thatched cottage as a gift. He sang the whole day to charm the bees. "They like that," he'd say, "especially the Queen Bee." But an old spinster of the region, Mademoiselle Blanche...

MANOLL: The Dame Blanche...

CENDRARS: No. I was going to deliver my honey to Dame Blanche, *boulevard Saint-Germain*, and my pears to **Potel et Chabot**, avenue Victor Hugo. I had no other clients; Those two alone bought up my entire production. You can see it wasn't very complicated as a business! No, Mademoiselle Marie Blanche was the name of my neighbour. She was a ghastly dwarf, with a beard right up to her eyes. She was an anarchist militant who spoke at conferences and wrote propaganda brochures on Malthusianism and defending child-mothers and the right to free love. Figure that, with such convictions, Mademoiselle Blanche would go mad with fury when you spoke in front of her about the Queen Bee. "The bees don't have a queen!" she would screech in her falsetto voice. "They're not that stupid! It's a prejudice propagated by mankind! Bees have only one mother, a girl-mother…"Mademoiselle Blanche had the finest hives of the region. She took care of them personally, and it was a real show seeing how this bearded dwarf, smoking her large beekeeper's pipe, with an enormous hat under which she virtually disappeared, tangled up inside the oversized, raw silk veil hanging from her face, her nude hands covered by bees who didn't sting her and who she called her dear little workers. All the proceeds from her hives went to the girl-mothers and other anarchist works.

MANOLL: Didn't you found an anarchist review somewhere around that time?

CENDRARS: I've never founded an anarchist review. I wrote in a free review…

MANOLL: Which was called?

CENDRARS: *Les Hommes nouveaux.*[10]

MANOLL: It was in this review that you assumed the defense of the Bonnot gang, I think.

CENDRARS: They didn't need me to defend them. I spoke of them with much sympathy. This story about the Bonnot gang was earth-shaking at the time. They were shutting the gates of Paris. Trenches were being dug out on the avenues, they…

MANOLL: You produced a special number…

CENDRARS: No, it was a series of papers. I knew several members of the Bonnot gang, Raymond la Science, Kibaltchich, aka Victor

Serge,[11] Armand, Rirette Maîtrejean, and the Russian, going by the name Dubois, a typographer at the *Imprimeries nationales*, the sole member of the gang who was never nabbed.[12]

MANOLL: Can you name a few people with their signature in your review?

CENDRARS: No.

MANOLL: Didn't you take the defense of André Suarès?[13]

CENDRARS: Yes, I did a piece on Suarès.

MANOLL: Why?

CENDRARS: Because he was unknown.

MANOLL: Wasn't his position in a way analogous with that of Remy de Gourmont? He was a person who charmed you.

CENDRARS: Not at all. André Suarès was no sceptic. He was an avid believer. He signed his anarchist leaflets *Res-Sua*. He was a militant. He distributed or sold his brochures himself. His was a philosophical anarchism a bit in the style of Prince Kropotkin. All these short writings have almost disappeared.

MANOLL: I understand.

CENDRARS: I wrote an unfortunate short piece on André Suarès, rendering homage to him. One morning, I heard someone climbing up the stairs, and then knocking on the door of my flat on *rue de Savoie*. An old peasant woman entered who had just arrived from the countryside that morning. Her grey hair visible under a headscarf, a basket across her arm, and carrying six apples hand-picked the same morning from her garden and now offered to me as a gift from André Suarès. "The master is so pleased," she said. "It's the first article that has ever been written about him…" I never could determine whether this good peasant woman was the governess of the writer, his wife or a former mistress. She was a very simple person coming from a humble background. But she was very clean and her hands were well-manicured.

MANOLL: I have heard that a lot of apples were brought to the literary circles of those times. I recall that Louis de Gonzague Frick[14] brought an apple to Apollinaire every morning.

CENDRARS: Poor Frick, lovely fellow. He might have done that once.

MANOLL: Was it during those times as a honey farmer that you met Antoinette, the daughter of the deep-sea diver?

CENDRARS: Of course, the unforgettable interludes with Antoinette!...[15]

MANOLL: You have related that: the long walks along the river...

CENDRARS: At the bottom of the river! Do you think that I wouldn't drink some plonk with Antoinette's father without trying their huge contraption and to take my own plunge to the bottom of the water?

MANOLL: You wanted to experience what it felt like to be a deep-sea diver?

CENDRARS: The hardest thing is to keep the head high. It's an extraordinary sensation. Even though you have fifty pounds of lead on each foot, once you're in the water, you lose your footing. The slightest mistake pushes you down twenty metres and you are head over heels. It's devilish to try and rebalance yourself. It's unbelievably amusing .

MANOLL: And Father François?[16]

CENDRARS: The horse-and-cart man?

MANOLL: Yes, the man who sold his stable to purchase one of the first automobiles...

CENDRARS: A real bone-shaker, that one, a rattle-trap!

MANOLL: Yes, Father François, who had parked the old renovated vehicles in a vacant parcel of land at Saint-Ouen, where he lodged the most miserable of the lowly rag-and-bone men of the region...

CENDRARS: Ah, yes, the caravan of misery...I've never seen anything else like it, not even in China...

II

Plundered by the Gestapo

MANOLL: Didn't your father design a hotel in Heliopolis,[17] one of the first palaces?

CENDRARS: As a matter of fact, he didn't just design it. He had it built in 1890.

MANOLL: You liked to turn on the bathroom faucets, so you could watch the small serpents and lizards slithering out with the water from the Nile.

CENDRARS: The hotel remained empty for twenty-eight years. There were no guests. Nobody was interested in Egyptian tourism. International tourism, *le grand tourisme*, hadn't yet been invented at the time.

MANOLL: With a father like yours who followed his impulses, you were often on the move.

CENDRARS: That we were.

MANOLL: Moving from Egypt to Italy, then to Paris, then on to London, sometimes staying in luxurious mansions, sometimes in hovels of the poor…

CENDRARS: What do you expect? My father was an inventor. That's what inventors do, invent. My father used to invent gadgets, let's see: crystal lettering for showcase windows, the first neon signs, the Roman chariot which raced from inside the façade of the house at the corner of *rue Taitbout* and *rue Laffitte* on the boulevard, slot machines. He had a hand in everything; he was boiling over with ideas. He was a dreamer and chronically agitated. He enjoyed tackling problems, big and small. He started out in life as a mathematics professor. He was very funny, a clown. At home, each door was equipped with a device which allowed it to be kicked open. Even today, my reflex is to kick rather than push doors open…He was ahead of his time, but he also produced things. He invented the first machine to automatically weave Smryne carpets, including the stop, this tuft of hair that the women workers knotted at the end of their ball of wool at the end of the day to mark the place where their work resumed the following day. He should have made a fortune solely with that unique invention. But as soon as he invented something, Papa had only one thing on his mind, and that was to move on to the next one, which of course meant that he never got around to generating any profits from his inventions, as he was already rushing out to sell his patents and liquidate his rights to procure some cold cash and fine-tune his latest brainchild. That's why he had so many highs and lows. Meanwhile, we'd catch it all on the rebound back home without ever really figuring out what the origin of all the trouble was. So, little by little, I turned to the street which of course had my mother at wit's end.

MANOLL: If we were to design your family crest, my dear Blaise Cendrars, we'd have to include a map of the world and an open book. I think that properly reflects your insatiable curiosity and your love for poor humanity, sentiments which rely not only on intuition, but on a universal communion with your fellow humans…

CENDRARS: My family crest? It already exists and goes back to the XIVth century. That's my family crest.[18] But, it's not as complicated as the one you are imagining, my dear Manoll. It's nothing more than a cross and a cloven foot on a shield. I don't know what it signifies, and it probably has more to do with cows than it does human beings, as it surely isn't a symbol of nobility. My ancestors also had to brand their cows [*pecus=pecunia*)] with a hot iron as I've seen done in Brazil on the ranch of Coronel Luiz Logrado[19] who branded his cattle (30,000 head) with a double L in capital letters, with the first inverted like the monogram of the King which appears hundreds of times on the façade of the Louvre "LL" in a crown of Laurier leaves.

MANOLL: Browsing through your books, you constantly come across phrases of this type: I read a lot, through sleepless nights and also throughout the day. You have read a lot in your life?

CENDRARS: Voraciously.

MANOLL: Voraciously…

CENDRARS: It's my passion.

MANOLL: Everywhere, under all circumstances?

CENDRARS: Everywhere under all circumstances and every species of book. I have devoured everything that has fallen into my hands.

MANOLL: How many languages do you speak?

CENDRARS: No idea: French, English, German, Italian, Spanish, Portuguese, Russian, I can jabber my way through ten or twelve others. But I only write in French.

MANOLL: What about your work habits? You said somewhere that you rise at dawn and that you work for several hours.

CENDRARS: I never forget that work is a curse. That's why I never wanted to fall into the habit of work. Of course, as a concession to custom, at a late stage of the game, after I turned fifty-five, I decided to work regularly on a fixed schedule, and I spawned four books in a row. So, now I've got a crushing workload. But that doesn't mean I necessarily have any work method. Actually, I did deploy one for a time, and it worked pretty well, that's true, but that's no reason to blindly stick to it until the end of my days. There's more to life than writing books.

MANOLL: You say that, but at the same time you are an extraordinary work-horse.

CENDRARS: You're the one who's extraordinary! You want people to keep writing books without ever stopping! Where does that all lead? Tell me…

MANOLL: Well, I wasn't saying…

CENDRARS: Go take a tour of the *Bibliothèque Nationale* and you'll see where it leads you, that whole approach. To a grave. Millions of volumes delivered to the worms. Nobody knows who wrote them anymore. Nobody even asks. Terra incognita. All very discouraging.

MANOLL: But, do you recall, Blaise, the times when you spent hours and days, even months in the Mazarine library, copying by hand the novels of the age of chivalry?

CENDRARS: To earn a hundred francs per incunabulum! Of course I remember! Even…

MANOLL: You were toiling for Guillaume Apollinaire!

CENDRARS: For Apollinaire, who was doing it for P.-P.P. who was doing it for Payot, the publisher. To the best of my knowledge, only one of these novels of the Round Table was ever published: *Perceival le Galloys*, in the *Bibliothèque Bleue* collection.[20] But I delivered a half-dozen ready-to-print volumes to Apollinaire: Lancelot of the Kake, Mélusine…

MANOLL: And, yet it was Guillaume Apollinaire who put his name on the cover!

CENDRARS: Apollinaire, yes. But also P.-P.P., Pierre-Paul Plan,[21] a real surly bastard.

MANOLL: And it was Apollinaire who gave you the hundred franc note?

CENDRARS: It's Apollinaire who, quite honestly, shared with me what he had received from P.-P.P.; at least that's what I surmise.

MANOLL: Reading for you was a way to travel, to vagabond through time and space, but as you have put it, to penetrate beneath the skin of a character with minimal effort.

CENDRARS: No, for me it was an opiate.[22]

MANOLL: That's why you have warned...

CENDRARS: I drugged myself on printer's ink!

MANOLL: You have warned against the perils of ink.

CENDRARS: I warned against what?

MANOLL: You spoke about it and you said it easily warps the progress of the soul, that it leads a reader astray.

CENDRARS: Ah! Of course, I was referring to people – and there's no shortage of them – who always think they're some reincarnation of a character out of a novel and as a result suffer all the morbid influence of reading, much in the way of a young medical student who auscultates himself neurotically, and who engages in self-diagnostics the way others read their horoscope and then imagines at every turn that he is suffering from every malaise he reads about in his books. It's classic.

MANOLL: You once were a medical student yourself.

CENDRARS: Bloody hell, yes, and I don't regret it! It was a regular lark studying medicine. It stays with you for a lifetime. You're never done with learning about and studying man, this hitherto unknown form of life. But, of course, you have to deal with the Faculty, the exams,...a damn curse!

MANOLL: You spoke earlier about reading as an intoxication. You have dissected and classified several types of reading addicts. In Chadenat,[23] the famous bookseller on the *quai des Grands-Augustins*, whose library at the Hôtel Drouot is being liquidated, already for sums in excess of twenty million, Chadenat is the type you call a pure reader.

CENDRARS: Yes, driven by passion. A man who managed to feed his vice. A man who set up his own bookshop. A man who had built up a bookshop so rich in rare and exceptional and rare books, even unique in the world, because he was depraved, a pervert and an addict, because he was a great collector. All collectors are depraved. Read your Freud. He drew his own conclusions.

MANOLL: According to your account, Rémy de Gourmont was a man suffering from moral vertigo, who read to create a zone of emptiness around himself.

CENDRARS: That's right. That's what I believe.

MANOLL: And, as for yourself, you'd classify yourself as…

CENDRARS: Yes, he was a unifier of words, but a disconnector of ideas.

MANOLL: Yes, and yourself…

CENDRARS: He even founded a review…wait… the Review of the Dis-assocation of ideas…the least you can say is that it's original.

MANOLL: Yes, and you classify yourself as being among the men who are mad for reading, just as Constantin Guys, in your own words, was mad about sketching.

CENDRARS: Or Goya. In fact, I intoxicated myself throughout my life, especially during my youth.

MANOLL: A book, you said, is a deforming mirror, an idealized projection.

CENDRARS: Oh! There are different theories. Every school has its esthetic. Didn't Naturalism claim that a novel was a mirror taking a stroll at roadside, to which the Impressionists retorted that it was rather a mirror strolling at the edge of a canal or a river? But, I recall Baudelaire's porter selling his merchandise in Parisian courtyards, simple glass panes, but much more fragile and marvellous and subtle than mirrors. You might even say magical mirrors.

MANOLL: You still can't deny your prodigious craving for the written word. You once recorded that in Peking, during a particularly calamitous time of your existence, when you were a coal-trimmer at the *Grand Hôtel des Wagons-Lits*, you stuffed the gravity furnace with editions of *Mercure de France* after reading them.

CENDRARS: Well, at least I read them prior to burning them. Like others do with newspapers in the WC: they read the paper before putting it to good use.

MANOLL: Whenever I see the heavy trunks of books piled into your rooms in the apartment where you currently reside in Paris, I recall those you transported with you during three voyages through Persia, China and Russia, filled with rare books.

CENDRARS: It was my great era of intoxication and I traveled by caravan.

MANOLL: You've always travelled around the world with trunks and trunks of books.

CENDRARS: No, no, no, no. That's finished. I couldn't possibly do it anymore. Try and bring a trunk of books onto a plane, see how much that'll set you back! That dozen or so trunks of books you noticed the other day at my place represents all those years of exile, my absence from Paris.[24] These are dedicated books that were sent to me by friends during the Occupation. It's not a library. In fact, it's the contrary of a library. The Krauts plundered my library.[25]

MANOLL: And, you didn't transport the others?

CENDRARS: No, except for two or three works that I need for pending or future works. That's all. The books were too cumbersome.

MANOLL: Let's return to your biography, to this final rupture with the bourgeois life you were forced to lead in Neuchâtel in Switzerland, one night during your sixteenth year on the planet, in 1903, I believe. This plan to run away from home, had you prepared it well in advance?

CENDRARS: What thing is that?

MANOLL: Your escape.

CENDRARS: Not on your life!

MANOLL: You didn't prepare anything?

CENDRARS: I didn't prepare anything at all. I flew the coop one fine Sunday morning, late in the afternoon, because I was fed up.[26]

MANOLL: You couldn't bear the shackles your father was imposing on your craving for freedom.

CENDRARS: Not on your life! Poor papa, he was the most tolerant man I've ever met in my life.

MANOLL: One wonders whether your mother, this strange and seductive creature, had she been alive, you would have avoided…

CENDRARS: What the hell are you talking about? My mother was alive! *Diable*, it's even the only thing that I regretted.

MANOLL: So, you fled the family home without any fixed plan.

CENDRARS: I left…I left because I felt like it and because the opportunity was there.

MANOLL: You left without a fixed plan and with no hope of return?

CENDRARS: How would I know? I left for the east because the first train coming by the train station was eastbound. If it had been a westbound train, I would have stepped off the train in Lisbon, and I would have discovered America instead of Asia.

MANOLL: It was an extremely important date in your life because as of that moment, your life can be divided into two phases: your adventures in the Orient and your adventures in the West. From that time onwards, you no longer had a roof.

CENDRARS: Those are things you say when you're spinning a good yarn…

MANOLL: Certainly, but…

CENDRARS: To put a little bit of order into your existence. But my life was never split into two parts.[27] That would be too easy. Anybody could split his life into two, into four, into eight, into twelve, into sixteen parts.

MANOLL: At any rate, what I want to establish is that during your escape, you weren't either possessed by the imp of the perverse or undergoing some emotional crisis.

CENDRARS: No emotional crisis.

MANOLL: No literary influence either?

CENDRARS: None.

MANOLL: You had the vocation to be a man alive, ready to break off, to create a rupture.

CENDRARS: If you like. But I don't believe a word of this.

MANOLL: You…

CENDRARS: I wanted to leave. I wanted to run away like a kid who is sick of going to school, who wants to escape. That day, I was punished, and since I was locked up, I jumped out the window. If the door had been open, I would have walked out the door, believe me.

MANOLL: You liked taking risks.

CENDRARS: How would I know? How could I know what to expect from life?

MANOLL: It's no accident that the title of one of your books is *In Praise of a Dangerous Life*.

CENDRARS: Yes, fifty years later. But, that's not my life. I think it's one of the rare books where I hardly talk about myself.[28]

MANOLL: You do, however, say in this book that the thing that goes most against your writing is writing.

CENDRARS: That's obvious. I developed a taste for the outdoors, for trips. I don't like being trapped up inside.

MANOLL: You also wrote a phrase in *In Praise of a Dangerous Life* which seems to perfectly sum up your approach to life: "Life is dangerous and the man who acts has to pursue his act to its logical end, without complaining."[29]

CENDRARS: It's true. But, it's not me who said that. I was just faithfully reporting the statement made by a prisoner one day when I was visiting a Brazilian prison, deep up country in Brazil, or more precisely at Tiradentes, the city of the tooth-ripper.[30]

MANOLL: Febronio?

CENDRARS: Ah! No. Not Fébronio.[31] Indio Fébroniodo Brazil is a Brazilian Negro locked up for life in the *manicomio* of Rio, because there's no death penalty in Brazil. The man whose phrase I borrowed was a white man. He was a Dutch Brazilian, a railroad manager who had sliced open the chest of his rival with a knife, tore out his heart and ate it raw, sank his teeth right into it. That's why he said that you have to go to the logical end of your act, without complaining. He didn't complain. When I ran into him, he'd already served twenty-five years when I visited him inside. I asked him: "Tell me, if you were released today, would you recommence?" "Of course, I'd pick up where I left off," he said with a smile of morose delectation. Up until that day, I still hung onto the belief that prisons were there for a reason. But his response proved to me that they serve no purpose whatsoever. We can tear them all down in all serenity. There's only the soul of man that counts. Walls and irons are all for show.

MANOLL: Tell me, Cendrars, is it true that you were a whale fisherman? Whether or not you did, there's one in *Dan Yack* who took raw delight in hooking whales?

CENDRARS: You've been taking a long detour to bring me back to *Dan Yack*, aren't you? You won't let me out of here without dealing with that.

MANOLL: Makes no difference to me.

CENDRARS: Of course not. I was in love with the daughter of the King of the Whale-fishers. She was the reason I managed to get on one of the boats.

MANOLL: It was an American, naturally?

CENDRARS: Since the end of the other war, i.e. for the last thirty-plus years, the kings of the whale fishers are the Norwegians.

MANOLL: Ah! Norwegians, you say? So, this girl must have been a splendid blonde with braids?

CENDRARS: Not at all. She was a dark Nordic. After the Basques, who became adept at whale fishing already in the high Middle Ages and who arrived each season in Spitzberg to cast and burn their catches on the ground, the French aces, whose fishing campaigns often lasted two or three years, hunted whales on all the seas of the globe throughout the 18th century, when they were replaced almost exclusively by American flotillas from Norfolk (Virginia). In modern times, the whale catchers, hunting down the whale with harpoon cannons, were mostly Norwegians, and they committed such ravages, even ravaging the ocean floor, that today they're obliged to hunt prey as far as the Antarctic Ocean. Their centre of activity is at Port Deception, where the boat-factories are anchored so as to triturate whales on site using perfected tooling for the purpose. There's hardly any waste.

MANOLL: What's extraordinary is the phenomenal number of whales taken ever year. I've seen some statistics…

CENDRARS: I don't have the figures.

MANOLL: Thirty-eight thousand whales!…

CENDRARS: I don't have the figures, but I think you're exaggerating. I estimate around 15 000 whales per season are killed. At any rate, it's a catastrophe, because whales are an endangered species. You can't find North Atlantic right whales anymore that are 125 metres long, such as the one described by Buffon, which he measured against *Notre-Dame de Paris*. That whale was far higher than the towers of the cathedral. Today, when you draw a whale that is 20, or maximum 25 metres, you've snared a calf. The calf no longer has the time or the space necessary for its growth. It has to grow to an old age. For a whale to reach full maturity, you need ten centuries. But, they've been hunted down so ruthlessly over the last thousand years that whales have sought refuge in impossible locations like the seas around the South Pole, where the Norwegians track them down, as I told you, with cannon shot. They even harpoon the Sei whales, the Gibbar, the Minke Rorqual, the humpback and other crap, muck and offal of baleinopterides that they previously used to throw back into the sea.

MANOLL: Do you still read the books of Captain Lacroix?

CENDRARS: I've read them all.

MANOLL: Who exactly is he?

CENDRARS: He was an old seafarer and his books are a real feast. I never had the luck to meet him. I looked for him in Nantes, in Saint-Nazaire. They told me he was eighty years old and that he refused to abdicate. Since he couldn't sail anymore, he recycled himself as a maritime insurer. I've heard he doesn't hesitate to put on the belljar to investigate *in visu* the damage in the hulls. At his age, it's pretty admirable.

MANOLL: No doubt.

CENDRARS: I would imagine that those winter evenings in front of the fireplace must seem long to him, when the wind from the sea flushed through his village on the Lower Loire and surged right into his chimney. I guess it's probably to kill time that this man, who has criss-crossed the Seven Seas on board just about every type of vessel possible and imaginable, set down to writing books. They are thick books, solidly built, fortified by solid documentation, sometimes a bit dense, but almost always unedited, so never fastidious. Particularly since the old seaman even inserts items like illustrated postcards, and photos of his wild escapades during the time of his youth. He tells how everything came to him and everything he saw from Cape Horn to the seas of China, from Tasmania to Ouessant. He talked about everything. Lighthouses, currents, the wind, reefs, tempests, crews, the maritime traffic, the shipwrecks, the fish and the birds, the celestial phenomena and the maritime catastrophes, the history, the customs, the nations, the people of the sea, recounting thousands of anecdotes, familiar or dramatic, his entire life as an adventurer, carried along by the movement of the sea and dominated by his exclusive love for boats. Ah! Certainly, it's not a work of a man of letters. His pen is like a grappling hook and each page delivers up something. And these are enormous tomes! It's both very moving and simple as bonjour. In a word, it's miraculous. You touch the globe with your finger.

MANOLL: Among all these books on the fringes of literature that you like, can you cite me a few others?

CENDRARS: What, Captain Lacroix isn't good enough for you! Trust me, read him.

MANOLL: Yes, but still, what have you discovered since? What are you reading right now?

CENDRARS: The last book I discovered is the *Grand Dictionnaire de l'Administration des Douanes* that we owe to a decree of Vincent Aurio, then Finance Minister, and that I'm currently boning up on. It is titled *Répertoire général du tarif* and was published in 1937. Two volumes in-4°. Weight 50 kilos. I carry it everywhere with me because I'm going to need it soon when I finally get down to writing *La Carissima*.

MANOLL: Ah! *La Carissima?*...

CENDRARS: It's the tale of the mystical life of Saint Mary Magdalen,[32] the sole woman who ever managed to make Christ weep.

MANOLL: And you need the Customs tariff to write that?

CENDRARS: *Mon cher*, it's a question of language. For several years, each time that I set down to write a book, I first draw up a list of the vocabulary that I'm going to deploy. For example, with *The Shattered Man*,* I drew up a list of 3000 words in advance, and I used every last one of them.[33] That allowed me to gain a lot of time and conferred a certain joy to my work. It was the first time that I used this system. I have no idea how it came to me.

MANOLL: How curious!

CENDRARS: It all comes down to words. Words seduced me. Words

---

* *l'Homme Foudroyé*

perverted me. Words deformed me. That's why I'm a poet, probably because I'm sensitive to words – correct or incorrect, makes no difference to me. I'm either ignorant or don't care enough about grammar, which is on the verge of extinction, but I'm a voracious reader of dictionaries and if my spelling isn't too good, it's because I pay too much attention to pronunciation and the idiosyncrasies of a living idiom. In the beginning was not the word, but the phrase, a modulation. Just listen to the birds sing!

MANOLL: You said that in *Aujourd'hui* where you devote an entire chapter to words, and it's said that there are stenographic notes taken during one of your lectures abroad.

CENDRARS: I'm not a travelling salesman who is coming through town to hawk wares; I hate giving lectures!

MANOLL: You don't have to convince me. I can't really see you expounding in front of a green carpet while draining a flagon of water. But you're on record as having lectured at a conference in Sao Paulo.

CENDRARS: I've given five or six in my life. In Sao Paulo, someone in attendance recorded certain passages that she was kind enough to forward to me, and which I used in my essay on language. But it wasn't a lecture – more an improvisation on contemporary poetry.[34]

MANOLL: You have said that language isn't something dead, ossified, but rather something which is always in movement. Something fugitive which is always connected with life and reality.

CENDRARS: That's why the *Grand Dictionnaire de l'Administration des Douanes* is something I find so engrossing. For example, just take the word "ribbon". I have learned with stupour just how many meanings that the word "ribbon" can represent and especially its ultra-modern, industrial evolution: there's twenty-one pages on that alone!

MANOLL: I haven't forgotten that I am in the presence of the poet Blaise Cendrars and I would like to ask you why you haven't pursued this experiment that you commenced with "Easter in New York", "*Le Transibérien*" and "*Le Panama*"? There's a tempo to this poetry that you abandoned later on, particularly in the *Nineteen*

Elastic Poems that inaugurated an entire new poetic technique.

CENDRARS: I said in 1917 that I had just written a poem which stupefied me by its amplitude, by its modernity, by everything that I put into it. It was so antipoetic! I was in a state of ravishment, ecstasy. And at that moment, I decided not to publish it, and to leave everything that was modern poetry wade in its own waters and figure it out without my help, to see what would come of it. I barricaded this unpublished poem inside a trunk, this chest. I stored it in an attic out in the country, and I waited ten years before pulling it out and publishing it. That was more than thirty years ago, and I think the time still hasn't come to publish it.

MANOLL: The poem I'm talking about is "At the heart of the world".*

CENDRARS: Yes, and although it's unpublished, it's famous.[35] The other day, an editor offered me a million for it. I turned it down flat…

MANOLL: In your series of poems which follow the "Nineteen Elastic poems", there's a volume that you titled *Kodak*. If you gave it that title, it's that you wanted to say…

CENDRARS: Verbal photographs…[36]

MANOLL: They're verbal photographs, a sort of cinema, travel photos…

CENDRARS: Not of travels, of what I had under my eyes, what I was thinking, what I was divining, the verb…

MANOLL: In *Roadmaps*…

CENDRARS: Those were postcards I was sending to my friends, that I was shipping to friends…[37]

MANOLL: That's right, that's it…

CENDRARS: …that were destined for friends, that's why there's a lot of small stories not trying to be anything, but very intimate, particularly the portraits of people…

---

* *Au coeur du monde*

CENDRARS SPEAKS

MANOLL: Countries as well.

CENDRARS: Countries as well.

MANOLL: Life on board, people you met…In fact, I don't think you're going to let things stand, and I…

CENDRARS: I told you the other day that I've stopped writing poetry.

MANOLL: I don't believe it!

CENDRARS: I compose poems. I make poems for Bibi, I recite them to myself. I taste them, and they're delectable. I feel no need to show them to anybody, not even to people for whom I have a great affection. It's quite out of the ordinary when I cite one of these poems, even in a letter to an intimate friend. No, actually, that has never happened…

MANOLL: You certainly have stored them in your archives; you slip them into your files.

CENDRARS: Not at all. I don't even write them. It's so agreeable to daydream, to stammer out your private thing, something which remains a secret for yourself. It's a private vice.

MANOLL: Let's hope that one day…

CENDRARS: The problem when one writes, what grates now when I write, and I keep coming back to this all the time, writing goes against my temperament…dreaming up a novel, finding a subject, creating characters around the subject, having them grow in front of you, leading them, letting them participate in the action, mixing them up in all kinds of real-life adventures, all that is droll and amusing, a passion, and fits perfectly with the sloth that comes naturally to me, but the day when you start transfusing that into black-and-white, on paper, that's when I start suffering.

MANOLL: But, still, you spoke of one of your most ecstatic nights was a night of writing.

CENDRARS: No, no, no, not one of my most ecstatic nights of writing, an ecstatic night of love…[38]

MANOLL: So, not all nights writing are happy ones?

CENDRARS: Writing…it's such a bleak, thankless and actually, in all sincerity, you derive very little satisfaction from it. It's very unusual to say to yourself: 'That, old Blaise, *c'est pas mal torché*, you might even say it's good.' This type of badge of self-recognition is awarded on a rare day, I'll tell you.

MANOLL: Blaise Cendrars…

CENDRARS: …because what you see more than anything when you publish a book, when you look at everything you've missed, everything you didn't get inside it, everything you were dying to put inside the book, everything you want to add to complete it, because you see, it's so difficult to encapsulate things and to say everything with words. Once the book is finished, so are you. The disappointment is inevitable.

MANOLL: Blaise Cendrars, I want to thank you for granting these hours to interview you, which I find extremely agreeable and which I am also sure will be profitable for our listeners.

CENDRARS: Don't thank me, Manoll, you're the one who had the idea for these radio interviews. As for the listeners, I don't know if they'll derive much benefit. I've said it before, writing is possibly an abdication, but speaking…and talking about yourself!…and to the public!…where the hell does that get you? It's true that there is my voice, and solely a voice comes through over the radio, whatever it says. But I'm not familiar with my voice. I'm not an orator. I have never taken diction courses. Nobody has ever placed my voice on my lips. I discover the crackle of my voice coming through the microphone at the same time as your listening audience. I find it all very moving, but it disturbs me…It's crazy…

III

Picasso doesn't have a clue

MANOLL: Blaise Cendrars, the other day you were talking to me about the whale. What impression did you get of this mammoth beast?

CENDRARS: An impression of lightness, of agility, of vivacity. A whale that comes to play around a boat dives, tacks, sprays and sprouts foam, passes from port to starboard, scratches his back against the keel. It's an extraordinary spectacle, and when you reflect on the speed at which this enormous mass swims, and the grace with which it swims and dives. On a fair day, a pod of whales gliding across the path of a trans-Atlantic passenger liner in a convoy has all the appearances of a royal gala. Imagine the grand fountains of Versailles, a thousand spouts of water, a thousand wakes unravelling like ribbons, an entanglement of ripples, the sky aquamarine like an engraving.

MANOLL: You, who are versed in the Church fathers, tell me what is the symbolism, in your opinion, of the history of Jonas in the belly of the whale?

CENDRARS: I haven't the slightest idea. I am an ass at performing critical analysis. It really all comes back to language. If I read a tome from Migne's *Patrology*[39] each year, it's so I don't forget the vocabulary of the Fathers. My curiosity doesn't go any further. You'd have been better putting the question to Igor Stravinsky.[40]

MANOLL: What, Stravinsky looks into these matters?

CENDRARS: Actually, quite a lot. He's come up with things that have frequently surprised me. I have no idea why he engages in the practice. I do it out of love for poetry.

MANOLL: More than, say, out of love for whales.

CENDRARS: Sure, you could put it that way.

MANOLL: So, Stravinsky was an enthusiast of Christian symbolism?

CENDRARS: Yes, an aficionado. He could recite all the orthodox saints and the entire litany of Latin saints. One summer, I brought him along to visit the old Romanesque churches in Limousin. As we arrived, he spotted a statue perched at the summit of a church roof and identified the figure. He could tell you right away who it was, and he never got it wrong. It was astonishing. It still strikes me as incredible.

MANOLL: Let's go back to Dan Yack,[41] the famous Dan Yack, who I'm always trying to interrogate you on. Was it an important book for you?

CENDRARS: Of course.

MANOLL: It's an extremely important book to which you are extremely attached?

CENDRARS: For me, it counts primarily from the standpoint of writing. I used a form of writing which even surprised me. I had descended so far down into the inhuman atmospheric reaches where I had him living, Struge Island, the blizzard, the Arctic flora and fauna...

MANOLL: On the ice floe?

CENDRARS: Exactly...to a point that my phrases started freezing up and cracking. Sometimes they'd melt or lose their balance, turn on their heads, exploding, unhinging and drifting off to sea, grinding like ice floes crushing against each other on the Arctic sea. I think that all of that is well-rendered.

MANOLL: Some say the story symbolizes modern man. Is that what you wanted to convey?

CENDRARS: No, why, do you really believe this story about the symbol of modern man?

MANOLL: Would you rather I ask you whether you wouldn't prefer to be working in sales and marketing for a brand name selling canned whale-flesh?

CENDRARS: Sure, why not? On the other hand, In his study of me, Louis Parrot made a connection between the fate of Arthur Gordon Pym and the fate of Dan Yack.[42] I confess that I was surprised. I hadn't thought of that. I think that it is extraordinarily intelligent on his part. This unexpected parallelism inviting one to compare alphabet primers to runes had me musing. I suppose that Parrot must have been thinking of the alphabet primer of Paquita in L'homme foudroyé (The Shattered Man), the runes and dolls. It is so rare that a critic reveals something of worth to the author. Oscar Wilde said that when critics disagree, that proves that the author knows what he wants and is in accord with himself and the scope of his work. I'm in full agreement with this witticism and I would even add that you never learn anything from critics! That's why the conclusion of Louis Parrot hit me so forcefully. It was the first time something like this had happened to me ever and frankly, it stunned me. I didn't know Louis Parrot, who I had only spotted once, and that was in the push and shove of a cocktail. Poor Louis Parrot, such a lucid lad. He died while he was putting the final punctuation to his work on me. I had just the time to send him a telegram thanking him, and I don't even know whether he received it. I only received one letter from him, his covering letter...It was quite distressing.

MANOLL: I knew Louis Parrot well. I can tell you he had a remarkable mind, in full evolution. His premature death was a massive loss for the world of letters. But tell me, Cendrars, the human community that you establish there, in Antarctica, Community-City, a city with all the modern comforts, is this a foreshadowing of communism?

CENDRARS: It's not a foreshadowing of communism. During the same era, around 1930 (*Dan Yack* was published in 1929) the Soviets had started constructing an entire series of cities in the North of the Arctic circle, mysterious cities which already intrigued the Americans and excited their admiration, ports established along the Siberian coast, looking over the White sea and the Arctic sea, frozen ten months per year up to the North-West passage. Like me, who imagined an establishment out in nature where an agglomeration of humans had never attempted to survive, the Russians were inevitably forced by the logic of the matter to come to the same designs as I had, in no small part because it would be impossible to do otherwise in this climate and on land which is so precarious.

MANOLL: And the three characters in your novel who end up renouncing their vocation?

CENDRARS: Artists...

MANOLL: Didn't you say yourself that you fortified yourself in love and in solitude?

CENDRARS: In fact, artists live on the side, on the margins of life and of humanity. That's why they are either very grand or miniscule.

MANOLL: On the margins of humanity? Well, by that definition, you don't qualify as an artist.

CENDRARS: No. I have had thirty-six careers, and I'm ready to start again tomorrow morning, to start something completely different.

MANOLL: You've often said that, but you have been unable to escape from writing. No matter what you say.

CENDRARS: No matter what they say, you can't escape the very conditions of life, of course.

MANOLL: This need for expression is something which is marvellous.

CENDRARS: From time to time, of course you have to evacuate. It's like after a good breakfast, you have to evacuate. Remember the words of Christ: "Do not ye yet understand, that whatsoever entereth in at the mouth goeth into the belly, and is cast out into the draught? But those things that proceed out of the mouth come forth from the heart; and they defile the man". (Matthew, 15, 17-18). What can you do, it's neither a reason nor proof of genius to write compelled and forced. Madmen also write compelled and forced. You're not always going to hit the nail on the head.

MANOLL: All writers have complained about the constraints they suffer and the difficulty of writing.

CENDRARS: To make themselves look interesting, and they exaggerate. They should talk a bit more about their privileges and the luck they have to be able to bring to fruition such an artistic profession. I admit it's a profession I detest, but it's still a noble privilege compared to the majority of people who live like cogs and wheels in a mechanical set, who live as a function of this social engineering.

MANOLL: But, what about you?

CENDRARS: I wholeheartedly feel sorry for them. Since my return to Paris, I feel only tenderness, as never before, for the anonymous crowd that I see from my window, being engulfed by the metro, or coming out like automatons at pre-set times. Truly, it's not a life. It's not human. It has to stop. It's slavery.

MANOLL: You have expressed your compassion for them under all sorts of circumstances, each time that you have expressed your love for your fellow man, for the poor.

CENDRARS: Not just the humble and the poor, but the absurdity of life in general...

MANOLL: The absurdity of life?

CENDRARS: When a lad like myself, who believes in modern life, who admires all these beautiful factories, all these ingenious machines, realizes where it all leads to, he has no choice but to condemn, because, really, it's not very encouraging.

MANOLL: Yes, but still...what I mean is this need to write that possesses you, to which you surrender at such a cost...I'm thinking about the years of the Occupation during which the well remained absolutely dry, when you didn't write a single word.

CENDRARS: Nothing. Not a line.

MANOLL: That must have been extremely painful for you.

CENDRARS: I suffered, obviously.

MANOLL: It's not as if you remained idle. You were recording things without being conscious of it, since you ended up by publishing three books in short succession. The three books which make up your *Memoirs*, and are the most important that you have written.

CENDRARS: It's possible.

MANOLL: They contain extraordinary information on your life. But there is still more from this point of view, and I'm going to launch an attack on you.

CENDRARS: Be my guest!

MANOLL: Because you spoke earlier of your writing and you said that in Dan Yack you were surprised yourself to see how much your writing had transmutated. But your writing has undergone a continuous moulting. Take for example your essays in *Aujourd'hui*. It's right in the midst of "Esprit Nouveau". You disembark at Paris. I don't know whether it's the contact with the cubists, the futurists or the *simultanéistes*. In any case, your writing is extremely direct. You expose facts brutally. You are attempting to find a technical language similar to the lexicon of engineers. You…

CENDRARS: Don't talk to me about cubists, or any of those people, or the *simultanéistes*, or the abstract artists. I don't owe anything to painters.

MANOLL: It's your temperament, obviously, and you are a writer of temperament.

CENDRARS: These painters didn't have any influence on me. On the contrary, I'm the one who defended them. I argue, and I've always claimed, that a lad like Picasso, who claims he is the father of cubism, and generally all the painters of this school are fifty years behind what the poets were producing. A lad like Picasso did a marvellous job of illustrating Mallarmé: *A throw of the dice will not abolish Luck*, but since he hadn't really given the matter any thought, he was in fact illustrating the sonnets of Gongora! Which is to say no more than the other painters who believe they are the avant-garde of the contemporary world, Picasso doesn't have a clue about modern poetry. Painters have yet to attain the vision of Rimbaud. That's what I mean when I say they are behind the times. Of course, they exercise a vast influence on contemporary fashion, on the décor of life today, on this famous refined "French taste" which has always been the prerogative of the minor painters of Paris who seem to fortuitously fall onto the sword of their "discoveries". A Picasso only has his taste to fall back upon. Even when he's crumpling things together, when he's crumpling together faces, well! he threads and he creases and he crumples and he pleats. He's working for the fashion industry. He's not working for modernity at all and still less for life. His success, his universal influence, even his triumph proves that he is not a master. How else could you explain that all the snobs of the *Côte d'Azur* are suddenly adepts as if they're been touched by the grace of the gods of cubism. Painting has never been so ugly. It's basically aesthetics. A cubist friend told me on the eve of 14, and it wasn't Juan Gris, the poor bugger, who never could stomach the lot of them: "I don't know how the others do it. The more I pay for my colours, the more my painting disgusts me…"

MANOLL: You don't think that Picasso is a precursor?

CENDRARS: *Ah non*! He's the bastard child of the academics. His father was a museum conservator. He was fighting with his father, not with his creative demons. He was neurotic, governed by his complexes.

MANOLL: But, you once formulated a definition of cubism.

CENDRARS: Yes, and it was an intelligent one. But I don't remember what it was, it was so long ago!

MANOLL: You don't recall, but at the time, you were right in the middle of it.

CENDRARS: Yes, I published articles in *La Rose rouge,*[43] in 1919, articles on painting and cubist painters, who were all my friends and who at the time really had it in for me, so when these articles appeared, because I announced the end of their school, the disintegration of the "cube" and that we would finally be able to call painters by their individual names again, and we would be able to distinguish them from each other: Braque, Picasso, Léger, Delaunay and no longer deploy that miserable epithet "cubists". Today, these same painters, now that they have achieved glory, victims of their own success which in addition to celebrity, brings with it a spirit of competition, intrigue and secret jealousies, start backstabbing each other, encouraged by the black hands of merchants of canvasses and each of them reproduce, with exaggeration and solely for self-promotion, written excerpts concerning themselves from these contemptuous articles written about them thirty years ago, which I have never touched, nor even altered a word, and which today, in 1950, are being used as prefaces or "cut-out" pieces for albums reproducing the paintings of these Great Men. These photographic albums, in black-and-white or in colour, actually bring me a lot of pleasure, because monopolising the world of publishing as they do proves to me that modern painting has increasingly become a mere accessory for museums, libraries, university lecture halls, mobile bookshops, bars, cafés and before long will descend into cellars the same way classical music did under the influence of jazz, and, thank God, no longer counts for anybody, except as ambient noise. It's what Satie called music as décor. Nobody suffers anymore listening to music. I'm sure that before long, nobody will even look at painting and now that I mention it, it'll be high time! 100,000 km of paintings per annum!

MANOLL: You seriously think poets are fifty years ahead of the painters?

CENDRARS: For the poets of today, there's no doubt about it. Painters still haven't discovered Rimbaud. Do you know any good illustrators of the Illuminations of Rimbaud?

MANOLL: In my opinion, Rimbaud's genius is sui generis.

CENDRARS: So sui generis that all this critical attention devoted to Rimbaud, from Claude and Arthur Rimbaud's sister, Mme Paterne Berrichon, right down to the lowest of the low of the zealots and armchair critics, right? Until Rimbaud just up and left and fell silent. Just look at him, at the corner of the table of Fantin-Latour, this beautiful urchin, elbows on the table and who is biting his nails with impatience, just dying to tell the lot of them to bugger off and to shout MERDE! to all these fine-feathered Messieurs! Now, where do you think he lived at this time, Rimbaud?

MANOLL: In Paris.

CENDRARS: He was sleeping in the Senate. He was being lodged by Leconte de Lisle who was the librarian at the Senate. You can understand why he wanted to get the hell out of there. Not even Léon Bloy figured it out, he who said of poetry's bad boy "Rimbaud, a runt pissing into the Himalayas!" Outside of poor Lélian,[44] all of Paris took him for a depraved delinquent, a faggot. It's a scandal!…

MANOLL: You said that your life as a man began in 1917 "when I understood that the poetry coming onto the scene had given rise to a misunderstanding which was going to permeate the entire nation and then spread worldwide."[45] What exactly did you mean by that statement? What misunderstanding are you talking about?"

CENDRARS: I've already told you about that. In 1917, I left Paris without any hope of returning, after having locked up the manuscript of *Au coeur du monde* inside a trunk. I felt like a woman who wants to bear a child, gives birth, then leaves the father behind, raising the infant herself so she can do all the coddling and pampering, smiling gaga into the little bugger's face and watching him grow in solitude and finding her own strength in devoting herself to the child with blind admiration and infinite tenderness (it's a rare occurrence, but I know some who have done it and who are happy). I was happy. I was in love. Love is exclusive.

Quand on aime il faut partir...[46]

And so I left Paris. I abandoned Poetry. I was happy. I had survived the war alive and now I wanted to live. I'm talking to you about poetry. About the misunderstanding of modern poetry. I'm trying to tell you about the surrealists. There's not one of these adolescents or mama's boys who produced anything new. It's flea market *bric-à-brac*. Everything the surrealists have produced out of the prison of Dada can be traced back to *Les Soirées de Paris*, the final issue, published in August, 1914. Personally, I waited in vain for something of worth to come out of them. Something that had never been said. Something new. Like everybody, I have always given kids full credit, the benefit of the doubt. "Youth is a sacred calling...but it's the young who so ordain," observed Baudelaire, the undeceived. The surrealists have to go back to square zero. They have announced this a hundred times. They were overloaded with talent, the blighters. But nothing came of it; When Anatole France, this ancient grinning ogre, finally died, they spat on his corpse that they paraded around the streets of Paris, and they were so amazed with their audacity, because in addition to their talent, they had connections, these sons of families... on the same day they hurried over flat on their bellies to render homage to André Gide, who was a living cadaver; Even the glory of Gide dates from that day. May the devil drag him down to Hell..."[47]

MANOLL: You're going a bit far here, Cendrars.

CENDRARS: Do you find? I can assure you; I'm not making it up.

MANOLL: You're going too far.

CENDRARS: What do you want me to tell you about the surrealists? I barely crossed paths with those people. At the beginning, they came to see me in my garret, *rue de Savoie*: the gentle Philippe Soupault a very charming lad, who was very shy but who became irresolute. Actually he even lost his nerve:[48] the vassal André Breton,[49] who was already putting on those ubuesque airs of the self-important provincial who one day the nation would adulate…and he never really did extricate himself from this agitated, pre-humous, inchoate fame. Louis Aragon[50] actually was somebody who almost became a friend of mine. Also far and away the most intelligent of the three, the most delicate, the most elegant, but also the most fragile. I heard the pulse of poetry beating beneath those feverish lyrics of his. He was a rebel, and then he crossed the divide into hysteria. Soupault, once dragged the two others to my home. He wanted me to give a lecture on the *Dames de France*. I pointed him in the direction of Guillaume Apollinaire. He'd never heard of him. Apollinaire was thrilled to have the chance to hold forth and declaim in his full lieutenant's kit in front of the beautiful women of the world of high commerce and industry. And the lot of them in nurse's uniforms! The whole mess was absurd. But how could you hold it against poor Guillaume? Since his trepanation, his whole character became unrecognisable and Apollinaire lapsed into a childish vanity. But when André Breton bragged that he was a close acquaintance of Guillaume Apollinaire as he "was constantly in his company during 1917 and 1918" as he puts it in his most recent biographical notice in order to attract god knows what kind of vainglory, I laughed straight to his face, and I still say to him he's a bloody liar…

MANOLL: Oh yes!

CENDRARS: Yes, and it's disgraceful! At any rate, the behaviour of the surrealists disgusts me. Normally, I never would have allowed myself to spout out this invective if after Apollinaire, Max Jacob and others who can't speak because they're dead, André Breton hadn't tried to grab an exclusivity on Rimbaud and Lautréamont. I wonder how such a thing could be possible in a country like France and how he could be left free to decree by way of *oukases* and *prikaz* in a supposedly free Republic of Letters. Everybody is just kowtowing. There's reason enough to get bent out of shape for you! We were free men at the *Soirées de Paris*. Just a few poets shaking the coconut palm and taking the rag out of everything, plus each and everybody. The respect of officials wasn't asphyxiating us, and nobody took themselves seriously the way they do today. People knew how to laugh.

MANOLL: So, what do you think of Jean-Paul Sartre?

CENDRARS: I have no opinion of him. He's never sent me his books. But, you're wondering what I think of existentialism? Schopenhauer was the first to warn me about philosophy professors who, based on official teaching, meditate upon, write, think and draft manifestos. And Sartre is first and foremost a professor. Philosophical plays put you to sleep in the theatre. Sartre shows his theories as plays. Novels are either well or poorly written. Except for Sartre's. Sartre's are stuck somewhere in the middle. Every day since I returned to Paris, I kept running into these young adepts, and I wondered, how exactly are they existentialist? Is it because they put on disguises every evening to traipse down to Saint-German-de-Près in exactly the same way that their fathers used to dress up every evening to go off and parade with the rest of high society or to force their way into a private club? It's a trend that will pass, which is already on its way out. Is it really necessary that people be so bored!? …Cinema, radio, television? The truth of the matter is that very few people know how to live and those who accept life as it is are even rarer…

MANOLL: I don't know what can be said about this invasion of the literature professors, but one thing I can say for certain is that the movement of Jean-Paul Sartre has spawned no poets. They've produced zero poets. Not a single poet emerged alive.

CENDRARS: You're probably right. With one notable exception. Robert Desnos. Robert was a very chic type. I used to have a lot of laughs with him. We drank together in a bar where we met that I baptized *L'Oeil de Paris* (The Eye of Paris), because it was on *rue de Rivoli*, under the arcades, a hop, skip and a jump from the Concorde. You could watch Paris parade in front of you without moving from your barstool. Robert maliciously nick-named the place *Madame Zyeux*, because of the women who entered, just to go downstairs to the toilet and then leave again without ogling us back so they wouldn't soil their pissy, insipid dignity, which actually had us pissing our pants laughing, since we were already cranked up by the *prunelles des cerises à l'eau-de-vie* which we were guzzling by the jar, while we spat out the pits into the backs of these anonymous swishing skirts, buried in fur and in for a quick make-up pit-stop. Youki had no reason to be jealous; Robert was a merry companion. We never talked about "automatist" writing. On the two or three occasions I tried to question him on this morbid label the critics were constantly trying to paste to his forehead, he'd just wink at me and toss out the drollest see-no-evil grin. That's why I never bought into the medium Desnos, any more than I bought into the mystic Max Jacob. Robert Desnos was a great poet.[51] A real poet. Go re-read "Quartier Saint-Merri", Manoll. It's in the same vein as Villon. One came from the quartier Saint-Jacques, the other from Saint-Martin. Left bank, right bank. Same thing. Drink at the source. The small bistros of Paris…

MANOLL: And what's your take on the young generation of the 1950's?

CENDRARS: The young can drive me to despair. And, now they're writing to me! When I was young, no young people wrote to me, which was fair enough, because I was young. Young people write me today because they take me to be an old man, and that saddens me, despite my age. But, finally, let's leave that aside…I confess to you that there's an entire generation of very young poets who are not yet published and who write me. I receive three, four sendings of poems per day, and from time to time, a leaflet. Unknowns…

MANOLL: Do any of them have any talent?

CENDRARS: Some young people have talent, some have no talent.

Some have genius; some are lacking genius. *C'est la vie.* They manage to get to me, and I always write back to them. But if they're writing to me with the intention of choosing a master, they've come to the wrong address. I'm not a school principal. I'm not old, fossilized, ancient to that point...it's lunacy...

MANOLL: But, since you don't accept your status as master, but you have had masters yourself; there are writers who have deeply affected you, and poets who have profoundly influenced you. It is said that Baudelaire is the father of modern poetry. From him, two schools can be said to have emerged – one formed of artists of the verb, like Mallarmé and Valéry and the other of poets who departed on the adventure of conquering the modern world..

CENDRARS: I'll leave Mallarmé to you, but Paul Valéry, this epigone who reaped all the honours more rightly due to his master, up to and including a national funeral, and the surrealists didn't protest! As for Baudelaire, of course I was influenced by him. He is a major poet, but above all, he was a profound, Catholic mind in his critique of modernity. As a critic, he was an astonishing figure, well ahead of his times, and I believe for a long time yet, say, right up to the end of the twentieth century, he'll influence young men by his critical stances and by his dandyism. His most beautiful lines are already landmarks. I place myself under the sign of François Villon.[52]

MANOLL: Another who seems to have considerably marked you, at least to the extent that someone like you could be marked, because you are not a man who is influenced, but a man who subjugates others to his influence, and many contemporary writers are influenced by you...

CENDRARS: This is horrifying! Stop this!

MANOLL: There's nothing you can do about it. "Easter in New York", the "Trans-Siberian", "the Panama", the...

CENDRARS: Tell me, since when have they been talking about those?

MANOLL: ...nineteen elastic poems...people are talking about them, and they're cited precisely because they form the basis of modern poetry, they're the foundation of modern lyricism.

CENDRARS: It's very good of you, Manoll, to say such kind things.

MANOLL: But, come off it, Cendrars, you are famous!

CENDRARS: Well, it's like the case of the cuckold, I'm the last one to know. No, no, not at all, I'm not the foundation of anything at all. It's the modern world which is behind it all, "enormous and delicate",[53] just like the Middle Ages. And the source, it's Villon. If they ever get around to publishing the correspondence of Max Jacob, you will find sources and foundations and departure and arrival points. And there's one who set out to shake the coconut palm until they all fall out *pell-mell* – the fake geniuses and the real ones, the pure and the impure. And he had a bad tongue to boot, and thrashed around like a succubus in holy water!

MANOLL: What, the honest ones too?

CENDRARS: He used to peel their shells away while roaring with laughter. You'll see. It's riotous.

MANOLL: I have difficulty in believing that.

CENDRARS: Poets don't have fun anymore. That's what guts me the most today – seeing how seriously they all take themselves.

MANOLL: It's true. We don't know how to laugh and very few things amuse us anymore. Sorry to admit it, but my entire generation is like that: we can't seem to laugh. But there are causes for that, obvious social causes, economic causes…

CENDRARS: Do you honestly believe our lives were a lark at the time?

MANOLL: They weren't?

CENDRARS: My dear Manoll, during the *Belle Epoque*, contributors earned one sou per line in the newspapers, and Apollinaire had to wait months and years before being able to sign his copy and count on a regular, paying collaboration. That's why he published erotic stories, for his bread and butter. You have no idea the extent to which doors were closed to us. I have the impression today that we are much more welcoming. I meet young people everywhere; In newspapers, on the radio, in the studio. Pre-14, those who wanted to were already lining up at the door, or for positions already closed off to them. The others were eating mad cow out in the streets. We didn't give a shit. We laughed. Parisians are a beautiful people.

MANOLL: Our generation had it pretty bad!

CENDRARS: Everybody had to eat it, that's the fate of young generations. Luckily mad cow exists and it hasn't yet been canned for export like ape-flesh or corned beef. It's set aside for French youth so they can keep up the tradition of being *débrouillard* self-starters. One piece of advice: when you see an open door, journal, radio, studio, cinéma, bank, *eh bien*! don't go inside, or by the age of thirty, you'll be gaga, because you'll have left laughter at the door. That's my experience. Poetry is in the street. It goes arm-in-arm with laughter. It takes it out for a drink, to the source, in the neighbourhood bistros, where the laughter of little people is so delightful and their dialects are so beautiful.

...Il n'est bon bec que de Paris

IV

The Birth of Brazilian Literature

CENDRARS: Hé ! Manoll, get that piece of paper out of my sight; I don't want to see it! What are you pulling out of your pocket? That's not in the rules. You know I set the conditions for our radio interviews: improvisation and spontaneity. Otherwise, if the questions and responses are prepared in advance the game has no sense in front of a microphone. If you want to do that, you might as well go take a course at the Sorbonne or hold a conference in the Hall of the Societies of Wise Men, and that's not really my style. You should know better.

MANOLL: I wanted to talk to you the other day about Gérard de Nerval when the clock ran out on us. I was thinking of him when I said that one man had certainly left his mark on you – Gérard de Nerval, both the man and his life. Maybe even more his life than the poet who was attempting to establish an equilibrium between the magical and the real world...

CENDRARS: Dreams and life,[54] what Goethe called *Dichtung und Wahrheit*.

MANOLL: You cited in one of your tales a quatrain by Gérard de Nerval. That's the one I had noted down. Bear with me while I read it:

> In the night of the tomb, you who consoled me
> Give me back Pausilipp and the Italian sea
> The flower that so appeased my desolate soul
> And the climbing ivy where the vine and rose inter-
> twine[55]

By citing this quatrain, Cendrars, are you implying that the theme of your tale was provided by Gérard de Nerval?

CENDRARS: Certainly, throughout my life, I have been profoundly influenced by the works of Gérard de Nerval,[56] but I would never allow myself to assert such a thing as categorically as you just have. As I said, this quatrain of *El Desdichado* is one of the secret keys to my tale. The story itself is meant to be an evocation of childhood memories, if I can put it that way. The reading of the work of Gérard de Nerval, and more specifically, *Filles du Feu*, is also a childhood memory. I was ten years old when my father gave me that book as a birthday present and I read it and re-read it on numerous occasions. I undoubtedly was heavily under the influence of Gérard de Nerval during that time, particularly from the point of view of popular songs. He has sketched out the story for the Valois tales, since I knew all the verses and stanzas by heart. Later, during another period of my life, when I took myself for a musician, I attempted to reconstitute the music of these songs and did some investigating at the Opera library. I uncovered several ballet scenarios and opera booklets, but no music of the songs of the Valois. I am indebted to Gérard de Nerval who inspired my love for songs and popular poetry. In all the countries of the world where I have travelled, I have always gone to great lengths to listen, to record, to note and to read almost exclusively popular music, poetry and literature, particularly in Russia, China and Brazil. Generally, when I disembark for the first time in a country, in a capital that I don't know yet, I do a round at the bookstores – the small bookstores of popular quarters – to see what the little people are reading. They read Alexandre Dumas, cloak-and-dagger tales, romances for the secretaries – secretaries the world over have pretty well the same mentality. But, there is also in each country a series of works that are exclusively reserved for the popular classes, such as *La Clef des songes, Le Langage des fleurs* and a thousand others. Although this type of door-to-door literature is no longer fashionable in Paris, in a country such as Brazil, on the contrary, which is a new, young country, everything appears novel and entire veins of the population who have just learned to read, today are discovering for the first time these stories of sorcery, werewolves, of the headless mule, la *Dame blanche*, phantoms, Black humour, romanticism, fairy tales, novels of chivalry and the round table, the collections of puns, pearls and anecdotes known as *anas* and the adventures of highway robbers, famous crimes of passion, a marvel that is no more peculiar or obsolete than the morass of pulp reading in countries which are far more developed, and which includes the detective novels in England, the great romantic films in cinemas worldwide, all of which forms part of the ancient and timeless patrimony of folklore, of popular literature.

MANOLL: But, in Brazil, isn't this folklore entirely taken from Black culture?

CENDRARS: Not at all. The literary folklore is originally Portuguese. The door-to-door hawker literature was imported from Portugal. By the way, it's the real foundation of the Brazilian national literature. Much more than the Brazilian works of academics, which until recent years have always been generally influenced by French academic literature, for example, the most recent generation of young writers of Brazil follow the new North American novelists of the inter-war period, who generally lived in Paris and generally surfaced in and around Saint-Germain-des-Près and Montparnasse: Hemingway, John Dos Passos, Henry Miller.

MANOLL: But the Negroes who were displaced, did they write?

CENDRARS: The displaced Negroes, which is to say, the slaves, didn't write. They were prohibited from writing and it is extraordinary that any of them learned to read or to write. Besides, they were prohibited from printing books in Brazil, as they must have come from metropolitan France. The first printing press was only created in Rio de Janeiro in 1818, under the Empire. Thus, the *Complete Poetic Works* of Grégorio de Matos (1633-1696) who was justifiably labelled the François Villon of Brazil – or the *boca da inferno* as his contemporaries called him, because his satires of colonial society were so violent, they were only printed in Rio in 1882. Up until this date, they were transmitted by oral tradition and handwritten copies that circulated within a certain class of society: the Bohemia of Bahia.

MANOLL: He was a Negro?

CENDRARS: No, at best, a dark-skinned mixed-blood, a *pardo*, as they are called down there. His parents had a sugar cane plantation and possessed one hundred and thirty slaves. He was lucky enough to read law at Coimbra, the famous faculty of Portugal. When he returned to Bahia, his mouth which rained curses and his infernal invectives earned him a return into exile in Angola, Africa, from where he returned more radical and enragé than ever, to set up at Pernambouc, in a residence under surveillance. Far from mending his ways, he led a life of drunken revelry and debauchery with the Negresses of the port. All his love ballads, and there are some exquisite ones, celebrate the black Venus. He died in misery, impoverished. Legend has it that he was buried, like the lowest of the low, with his guitar, his sole asset.

MANOLL: And the literature of Blacks?

CENDRARS: It was also transmitted by oral tradition. We have forgotten that in the cargo holds of these millions of beasts of burden – manpower – that these *Negro* holds were flushing out representatives of all the peoples of Africa, each of whom was variously valued by the slave merchants and the planters on the basis of his physical endurance or his social character, but also highly sophisticated Blacks, individuals such as blacksmiths, cock-fighting trainers, drummers , fetishist-healers, sculptors, storytellers, poets, vociferator-shouters, conjurers, priests and warriors, in a word, sons of nobility, who were sold pell-mell along with the rest of the human livestock. These individuals lost in the herds of slaves forced onto the plantations. These are the pariahs, stigmatized in History under the label of Maroon Blacks or *Busi Nenge*, "bush negroes" – because they didn't bow down, because they became fugitives, because they revolted, because they sparked mutinies among their own, because, in the eyes of Christian missionaries, they exercised too much of an ascendant on the spirit of their brothers, because these leaders were listened to, and never kow-towed under the whip. They endured the worst tortures without batting an eyelid, and in the eyes of their contemporaries, were seen as superhuman, because this elite took revenge, because some of them, it is true, committed the worst exactions on Whites and others preached, recollected, recounted stories, conducted initiation ceremonies, fought secretly, punished, reigned by terror and occultism. We're talking about several individuals – isolated, foreclosed, banished, tracked, outlawed, persecuted, marked, branded with hot irons. Colonial archives have only recorded the name or the popular sobriquets of those executed, tortured in the public square and those placed in stocks or who had a price put on their head. These criminals saved their people in exile. By their example and their sacrifice allowed the soul of black Americans not to perish notwithstanding three centuries of oppression, Jesuit reductions, physiological misery, a regime of forced labour, suspicion, ridicule, mockery, and in spite of the imposed baptism, to not be entirely severed from poetry and the religions of Africa. The spirit blows where it wishes. Is it not the directing mind and founder of Aryan racism, the Count of Gobineau, this contemplative of the coloured races, who placed the crown of Poetry on the cursed head of the Black man?*

MANOLL: All that is fascinating. But, tell me, Cendrars, why then are there no Brazilian blacks in your Negro Anthology?

CENDRARS: Oh! That's another story. I had conceived my Negro Anthology in three volumes.[57] TOME I: a compilation at the *Bibliothèque Nationale* of everything that was published on Black literature up to the 1914 war. Tome II: Compilation at the British Museum of everything that had been published abroad and that the Nationale doesn't possess. Tome III: everything I'd collected myself from the mouths of Blacks in Africa, in North and South America, and especially in Brazil. Only Tome I was published, and, believe me, it was no small matter to find an editor for a work that was so uncontemporary and voluminous right in the midst of the paper shortages of 1919-1921. Against all the odds, three editions have managed to hobble their way to publication to date, plus an American edition.

MANOLL: And the two other volumes?

CENDRARS: The Germans took care of that; In 1940, Tome II was ready to publish, and Tome III was at the galley-proof phase. The Germans arrived in June 1940, pillaging my cottage house in Seine-et-Oise. I've been told that there's nothing left. I haven't yet had the heart to return for a look. Let's drop the topic, all right?

MANOLL: Fine, But I'm curious to learn from you, Cendrars, how you managed to hear these *Negro* tales recounted firsthand.

CENDRARS: It was pretty straightforward, you'll see. C'mon, follow me to Rio. I don't know whether you have any idea what Rio de Janeiro is like? It's a capital of more than two million residents, an ultra-modern city, filled with skyscrapers, with rectilinear avenues and curved beaches which wind all the way to hell and back. Steep, rugged mountains, covered by virgin forests and tropical vegetation which form a belt to the city from behind, preventing its extension towards the interior, and in the centre itself, a chained, tormented relief of hills that torque the geography like a screw and cloister the various neighbourhoods. It makes driving virtually impossible by complicating it in an unimaginable way by creating turns and detours that wind and tangle their way to perdition. These are the *morros*, the most famous of which is the Morro da Favela, through which lost faubourgs and unlikely suburbs wind their way. You find yourself in the middle of brutal savagery. From there, depart a thousand improvised paths and trails that lead through a species of urban bush land at the summit of these bluffs and ridges where the Negroes dwell in their blue *casines,* living life their own way in full liberty, doing nothing most of the time, singing, dancing all night and celebrating their macoumba during ritual feasts. They practically never come down into the city, except for the carnival, and then, they are the masters! The prefecture, which has had plans drawn up to remodel the city, consulted specialists from the entire world to kill off two birds with one stone: demolish the *morros* and at the same time, get rid of this itinerant Black population by flushing out the neighbourhoods and re-establishing them in viable parcel lots prepared in advance. But, the problem remains insoluble because it exists on too large of a scale. They already abraded a first *morro* on the shore of the bay, the prettiest, the most picturesque, the Morro de Castello, which formed part of the historical portrait of Rio de Janeiro. The engineer who finally achieved this took ten years, employing gigantic sluicers to crush the granite and to perform this putlilation on the city. Others simply pierced tunnels to allow tramways and buses to pass through, and put the various quarters into direct communication with each other. The most recent, Le Corbusier, proposed constructing an immense iron viaduct, perched on the summits and linking all the morros, in a continuous bridge, with the upper deck exclusively reserved for automobile traffic, beneath which he apparently hung hundred-storey "sea-scrapers", in imitation of the gigantic bee-hives in the immense forests of the inlands, to surpass even the skyscrapers. The idea was amusing and pleased me. Unfortunately, the idea was impossible to execute for about a million good reasons which had never occurred to Le Corbusier, because my pal Corbu was a poet and not an urban planner, so he was horrified at the idea of having to deal with contingencies.

MANOLL: You make me laugh with your "sea-scrapers". But what about your Black* friends?

CENDRARS: I'm getting there. So, when you disembark in Rio de Janeiro, the eye is first of all drawn by the *morros* which overlook the city, covered by a tapestry of small blue houses and clotheslines. It's up high where you feel like going! But nobody ever goes there. Imagine, if you like, twelve hills of Montmartre which are marvellously exotic. People would say to me: "Cendrars, La Favela is a savage, brutal place. Don't go there. You'll be murdered." The prefect of Rio, who was a friend, offered to have me escorted by an agent of the police services, which I declined, of course. Here's how I figured out a plan to go anyways, make friends and free myself of my protectors. There is no people more filled with gentle benevolence than these Negroes of the *morros* and the metropolitan suburbs of Rio! Another friend, a young doctor, intern at the Prompto Soccoro hospital was on duty every night at the door, and once I called him, he'd leave with his ambulance, a small Ford which went everywhere, collected accident victims, suicide cases, women giving birth, sick children suffering from angina, fever cases suffering from a crisis of malaria or alerted by the yellow fever, the nightmare of Rio, the murder victims, the lunatics. I used to keep him company during his shifts and when he was called, I'd jump inside his car beside him and we would race around all night, going everywhere, which allowed me to penetrate deep inside these Negro suburbs near and far, where a white would never risk venturing, and especially not the Cariocas, who'd shake like leaves just at the thought of it. That's how I made friends very quickly with these Negroes. They saw right away what type of man was the "nice little one-armed Frenchman who was helping out the good doctor and knew how to talk to people". Generally, I was well-regarded, and received with this ceremonial that the negroes put into all things, even the poorest, and later, that allowed me to return on a regular basis, alone and whenever I felt like it, and to witness their musical sessions…

MANOLL: Music…

CENDRARS: Guitarists. Singers. I used to record the lyrics of their songs. Their naïve poetry is admirable. Nights under a full moon, there was competition and the black poets challenge each other. A rhyme, an image, a verse. It's always improvised…

MANOLL: It's always improvised, but the old theme of black magic is never far.

CENDRARS: For transparency, yes, and often under names that don't mean anything, and that are spontaneously invented. It's marvellous. There was also in Rio a mulatto whom I very much appreciated. He was the double of Max Jacob. He was just as lousy a dresser as our poet and possessed a cruel wit, catty and villainously mischievous like Max. I can't tell you his name because he was the lover of a society lady, and I wouldn't want to compromise his venal enterprises, as Brazilian women are extremely sensitive. He knew everybody in Rio and like Max, he could put you to sleep with his tales. But he was refined, intelligent, full of implied meanings, often perfidious, and just like Max, he couldn't stop gossiping. He took me everywhere in Rio, in all the watering holes of the red-light districts and to the sailor's bars in the outlying maritime suburbs, or to country balls on Saturday night and Sunday afternoon at the Cinéma-Poussière, downtown, an elite "Negro Club". That's how I met Donga, who became a close friend. He was a pure race African, a perfect Dahomean type, with a round face like a full moon, constant good humour and irresistible humour. He had genius, the genius of popular music. He was the author of hundreds and hundreds of *sambas* and the carnival choruses and refrains which were on everybody's lips, including *Le Bœuf sur le toit*. During our first meeting, having learned that I knew Darius Milhaud,[58] he had this kind word to say: "Since he used my music, tell Mr Milhaud, your friend, to send me a postcard. He owes me that at least, from Paris, and that will please me, since I now want to compose *The Cow in the Eiffel Tower*, to render homage to Paris, which I have yet to discover."[59] Ernesto dos Santos, aka Donga, had constituted a small, typically Brazilian orchestra with violas, small and grand flutes, clarinet, whistles, the *choucalha** and the *batuta*. He started to gain some notoriety and started giving shows with his little or-

---

* a kind of round copper container filled with iron filings and terminating in a rod to which a rotatory motion is given, thus producing a continuous rhythmical sound (from daniv.blogspot.fr)

chestra in certain hotels of the Avenida, where a Negro orchestra never would have been tolerated in earlier times. Success proved fatal, since to live and ensure success and work, from one day to the next, he started to surrender to the influence of American jazz, the music in vogue among the dancing bourgeoisie in those days. The direction of his orchestra, the play, the composition, even the improvisation and arrangement of his Brazilian music took on the flavour of American trends by mechanically incorporating North American rhythms. I fear that the fine popular Negro-Brazilian music, with its syncopic rhythms as if it is in suspension, can no longer be heard in the depths of Brazil in the lost villages of the sertao, where I recorded some of it. I had brought some records back. I feel real chagrin that they are lost; but, alas, when my cottage was pillaged in 1940, you have to understand, I lost all my books, all my papers, everything, everything. When I learned about this in Aix-en-Provence, where I laid low throughout the occupation, it was a real blow. But at the end of several days, I said to myself: "Just my bloody luck!" and still a mountain of work before me."

MANOLL: You were at Paquita's, in this castle...

CENDRARS: I had ten years worth of work in progress. Then I found myself in the path of the juggernaut. The Krauts showed up, taking care of matters, they did...What a humiliation!...When I started writing again, in 1943, I started writing the trilogy you referred to the other day, what you call my Memoirs, and which are Memoirs without really being Memoirs...

MANOLL: I spoke about *Bourlinguer*...

CENDRARS: That's the series I'm referring to.[60] I started up again on the left foot and on an entirely new path. I think that from the standpoint of writing, I went far enough in my own writing. From the standpoint of composition and execution, I mostly wanted to compress or eliminate the notion of time. What I mean to say is that in the composition, I factored in the relativity of Einstein, and in the execution, the technique of Jean-Sebastien Bach...[61]

MANOLL: No, that's not the counterpoint that flows from the central motif...

CENDRARS SPEAKS

CENDRARS: Counterpoint?

MANOLL: …which means your mind…

CENDRARS: Those words, the texts, are written a bit like music…

MANOLL: That's it, music! That's what I meant…

CENDRARS: For example, if you take Gypsy Rhapsodies, – the word rhapsody already indicates that it is a musical form – you can notice that every quattro has the same volume, i.e. that they each contain the same number of pages, and that between the four stories, there is a hidden thread which unites them, which reveals the theme and its developments.

MANOLL: You have only given the key for one, but for the others, you haven't provided it.

CENDRARS: I'll give it to you today. I wanted to see whether the critics could discover that all on their own. I was criticized for having massacred my stories. The critics are starting to catch on that something else is going on.

MANOLL: In *Sky*, for example, in the sidereal Eiffel Tower, the tale has a broad unity and this unity, it's obviously your memory, the remembrances that live inside you, that are your personal experience. Aren't you afraid that this constant recall of memories which graft themselves onto the story ultimately unsettles the reader?

CENDRARS: I don't think so.

MANOLL: Ah, you don't think so!

CENDRARS: I don't think it unsettles the reader.

MANOLL: Everybody has his or her own work methods.

CENDRARS: The result is nevertheless excellent. And that's why I stopped. When writing becomes a process, it no longer amuses me. Not only does writing horrify me, as I've told you many times, and I was forced to write at that time, as the occupation had just ended, and I'd just washed away the abominable stain of it, and no longer wanted to talk about it. So, I forced myself to write everyday, from a set time to a set time, and sure enough, with a bit of training, you inure yourself to breaking rocks. And, so when it eventually became a formula, a receipt, pre-cooked, it bothered me. I stopped. I abandoned ten volumes and I don't know if I'll ever take them up again, because too many people came to see me in Villefranche-sur-Mer over these last years, and they found the place so beautiful where I dwelled, so custom-made for me, that they pictured me remaining in Saint-Segond until the end of my days. The editors began proposing contracts so I'd write one volume per year, two volumes per year, three volumes per annum. It was all spoon-feeding. I would certainly have needed a Dictaphone or some kind of a recording machine. In the end, all that profoundly bored me and anyways, I had expended such an effort that I was in fact over-exhausted. This fatigue is useful to me. It makes me indifferent to the last book that I published, and I hope I don't fall back in the rut. Eighteen hours of typing per day. I have had it up to here…

MANOLL: Are you writing something now?

CENDRARS: I'm not writing. I came to see you in front of your microphone. But once I've finished this series of interviews, *eh bien!* If I go back to writing this year, which I still doubt, I'll write a novel, a real novel.

MANOLL: One of those you have already announced: *La Carissima, L'Avocat du diable, Les Paradis enfantins?* [62]

CENDRARS: No. None of those are urgent. I've started them all. Some are actually well underway. What I need to do, as I did for *Gold* that I wrote in six weeks, is to one day have the desire take hold of me or to be so desperate for cash that I cloister myself, take one or other of the partially finished drafts, and finish it off in a few weeks. But for a new work, a new creation, I have a magnificent idea, and this time, it will be a real novel

MANOLL: A novel, a real novel, like Mauriac?

CENDRARS: That old spinning top Mauriac bores me. Doesn't he have any friends to advise him to drop the talk about holy God in the 15 franc newspapers? He's a real tweeting Shrike, that bird, ready to jump onto anything that's shiny. If the newspapers were still selling for a sou, I'm convinced that he wouldn't shoot off his mouth so much. Think about it, almighty god for a sou, almighty god for the poor.

MANOLL: Doesn't that embarrass you to say that?

CENDRARS: No, it doesn't embarrass me in the least. I say it without malice or afterthought because everybody is thinking it. Now, where were we now?

MANOLL: You were telling me about your next novel, a real novel.

CENDRARS: Yes, a novel, where I won't make an appearance.[63]

MANOLL: Still, we'll find certain elements of your life?

CENDRARS: No, no, no, no, not at all. You won't find me. I'll write a novel-novel and I won't make an appearance, because there will only be one single character in my books: Cendrars! Actually, that's not bad! *Gold* is Cendrars. MORAVAGINE is Cendrars. DAN YACK is Cendrars. They're driving me nuts with this Cendrars! People shouldn't believe that the novelist is reincarnated in his characters. Flaubert was never Madam Bovary. He might have felt ill when he described the poisoning of Emma and showed the same symptoms as the moribund vomiting, that doesn't make him Madam Bovary, even though he believed it himself when he said: "Madam Bovary, it's me!" are you telling me this beefy Norman is actually a closet queen? I know that he had all the quirks and idiosyncrasies of a man of letters and that he didn't really renew himself very much. But, on the basis of that, to conclude... it's really a bit of a leap. The greatest danger for a writer is to be victim of his own legend and to fall into a trap of his making.

MANOLL: Cendrars the vagabond! Tell me then, Blaise, when are you leaving on your next voyage?

CENDRARS: I don't know. I wouldn't mind travelling to China, and failing China, to the Indias.

MANOLL: Wouldn't that get in the way of writing your novel?

CENDRARS: No. Between now and departure, a lot of time will go by, but I may well have gone to the end of the world. Going to the end of the world doesn't prevent me from writing. I even hope to write in an entirely new way. A writer who is alive has to renew himself. And going into exile only favours that.

MANOLL: How do you do that while you're travelling? Do you write on board in your cabin or solely upon your return?

CENDRARS: I enjoy long sea voyages and the unsurpassed life on board to turn my attention to writing. It's the apotheosis of indolence, a triumph when you can do absolutely nothing while on board, everything moves, the ship is sailing across the seas, the machine is knocking, the ocean is agitating, the wind blowing, the Earth is revolving and rotating along with the skies and the stars and the entire universe is rushing to open up and let you go by. I am never in a rush to arrive and I have tried dozens of times to persuade the ship captain to take his boat elsewhere than his port of destination. "No way of doing it, alas!" said an old Hollander once. For thirty years, every month I do the return trip Buenos Aires-Rotterdam as if I was the navigator. Impossible to change anything. The trajectory is set in advance, the schedule drawn up. I have to arrive on such a day at such a time, it's all traced out in advance by the Company which is master just under God, and not me. But the most boring, it is always the same persons who embark. It's always the same heads I'm obliged to have at my table, the same chargés d'affaires, the same diplomats, the same nabas, the same grand banker for the last thirty years, ah! I know all this only too well! If only I had the courage to follow your diabolical suggestions, to give myself a jolt and to head out in a new direction, to the East or to the West, who the hell cares! and to round the Cape, and cut down towards the South seas!…"

MANOLL: And you lock yourself into your cabin as often as possible?

CENDRARS: I've been trying to tell you, Manoll, on board, I don't work.

MANOLL: But when you work? You said it yourself, it appears that you draw a veil over the mirror.[64]

CENDRARS: Writing in front of a mirror is the height of narcissism! I could never do such a thing, even locked up in my own room. I don't have enough self-satisfaction to satisfy myself doing that. I think I would write more easily in front of a crowd, like Simenon risked in the hall of *L'Intransigeant*. Somewhere in his Journal, André Gide confessed he wrote in front of his mirror. He said that while looking intensely at himself, he found that he had the head of a man fatigued, harassed, whipped, world-weary, worn and torn. He didn't say he disgusted himself, and that's too bad, if he'd been disgusted, he could have done like me and broken the mirror…

MANOLL: Whereas you, you lock yourself inside your kitchen at Aix, or when you're in Tremblay, you…

CENDRARS: In Aix, I was forced to live inside my kitchen. It was the sole location where I could burn two or three sticks of wood so I wouldn't freeze to death. This war, the last one, the World War, is for me a memory of freezing to death. I have never been so cold in my entire life. That started on board a destroyer of His Majesty during a patrol on the North Sea, and that continued in the same manner throughout all the long winters which were all very severe. When I went out to do a tour on the Maginot line to get material for my reports during the "phony war", you could see these poor soldiers who actually were freezing to death in Lorraine barns and silos, everywhere, and like in exile in villages abandoned where you watched for the wolves and during my tour, in exile at Aix-en-Provence, trapped in my kitchen, I was cold, so cold that these old aristocratic hotels of Aix cannot be warmed up, even if you have something, and I had nothing…

MANOLL: You spoke earlier about Gide who wrote in front of a mirror. You said that writing was a projection of the mind…

CENDRARS: I could never write in front of a landscape…

MANOLL: All your friends do the same as you. They place their work table in front of a wall, and they write in the same manner: Rémy de Gourmont, Peisson, 'Serstevens…

CENDRARS: You could add Apollinaire, who also wrote in his kitchen and who had trimmed a small white wooden table and encrusted a Mansard snuffbox under his window. Guillaume adored this little corner and preferred to remain there. One day, he even had a ridiculous little adventure at this little table...

MANOLL: Oh! Do tell...

CENDRARS: No, nothing...I was going to relate a charming tale.

MANOLL: I'm all ears...

CENDRARS: No, actually it's not gallant; it's obscene. It wouldn't work on Radio. It's too bad, because all the friends of Apollinaire who have heard the anecdote had a good chuckle...

MANOLL: Yes, that is too bad...

CENDRARS: It reeks a little bit too much of skirt...

MANOLL: Ah! well...

CENDRARS: Generally, the writer is a recluse. Saint Jerome, on the fine engraving of Albert Durer, is in his cell. He is the patron saint of translators. A polygraphic writer. A lion meditating on his tranquillity.

MANOLL: When you write, do you give yourself a break sometimes, or on the contrary, are you chained to your work desk?

CENDRARS: Over recent years, I've always been chained to my typewriter, and that's why I'm so disgusted...until the next time, anyways.

V

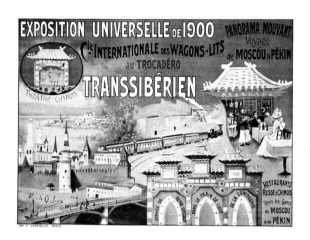

The Smell of the World

MANOLL: To get things started, I'd like to ask you a question which I'm pretty sure you won't want to answer, my dear Blaise Cendrars. Too bad, might as well risk it.

CENDRARS: As it turns out, my dear Michel Manoll, I happen to be in particularly good humour. You're in luck. You can ask me anything you like. And do you know why I'm in such good humour? Because I was waiting for a friend to show up at the *Aerogare des Invalides* and he stood me up. That's right. I stuck around for two hours, and for two hours, I watched the departures and arrivals of people disembarking from every corner of the world and leaving in every possible direction and for every possible destination, while my dear friend, my little Wagon-Lit was snoozing away! At one point, I woke up the hound with a good rough kick in the butt and

I told him: 'Listen, old man, for once that you have the chance to use your flair, go for it, and record and remember the various odours of the world!"

MANOLL: Smells, odours play a very important role in your work. For example, the Mediterranean…

CENDRARS: That depends; sometimes it has the good smell of a clothes closet. It was Rouveret, my friend and illustrator[65] who said that, and he added: 'Those things drop anchor in the mouth of a sailor, it penetrates so deep!' Rouveret was a former seaman. So, he knew what he was on about. But the Mediterranean can also smell of jam. In the Strait of Messina…

MANOLL: What is the smell of an airport for you?

CENDRARS: I couldn't detect it earlier today, because the odour of petrol was a bit too strong, i.e. motor vehicle petrol, but as for my dog, who from his position can sniff at the legs of people as they disembark or depart, it probably smelled like a bouquet, the bouquet of the world, the lucky devil. Certainly the passengers from the aircraft from Brazzaville or from Nairobi brought with them an odour which was different from those coming from Switzerland or from England. I'll go back as often as I can to the Air France airport, and to Orly and Bourget to see people from the entire world taking flight. I wonder when the first trip to the moon will take place.

MANOLL: You're getting the itch to vagabond again?

CENDRARS: No. I'm not dying from the desire, but I'll definitely be leaving again…

MANOLL: You're only making a temporary stop-off?

CENDRARS: I was thinking of leaving in a few years.

MANOLL: For the Indian Ocean?

CENDRARS: When I turn seventy. I'll sign up with Cook. I'll reserve a fine elephant, very calm and wise. Then I'll visit the wonders of India, the temples and Bénarès as an old gentleman being pushed inside a small wheelchair by a lovely registered nurse, with round firm breasts and a severe uniform, who will monitor me very closely to see that nothing happens to the old man placed in her care. One day, I'll trick her and perform a disappearing act and blend in with the natives, disguised as a pilgrim. And at my funeral, my hypothetical nurse will mournfully eulogize: he went native!

MANOLL: This appetite for travel, this insatiable appetite for travel is something which is absolutely incurable.

CENDRARS: I think it's incurable.

MANOLL: It comes to you from this long line of ancestors who wandered the entire world – your seven uncles, whom you referred to in your poem, *Le Panama*.

CENDRARS: Could be, but there's also a line of others, those who didn't roam about, ancestors who nobody talks about, and who were peasants.

MANOLL: What, there are still others in addition to those you refer to in *Le Panama*?

CENDRARS: Of course, and there were quite a few of them. My family originally came from a small Swiss village[66] which I visited for the first time of my life the other year to get married. It was Raymone who came up with the idea that I should visit my native land. I took advantage of that to carry out some research in the archives and I found ancestors in the fifteenth, and even the fourteenth century, where you can find my family name in perfectly legible letters on the most ancient document of the commune, dated 30 July 1347. All solid citizens, peasants, wine growers, councillors, judges, notaries, school masters, court registrars, who never budged from their alpine village of the Bernese Oberland, one of the best governed countries of the world, and where each, outside of official or non-official functions that he may assume, is first and foremost peasant, cattle herder, cheese-maker for the remainder of his life. The first time my people went into exile was in 1765, following the phylloxera that was ravaging the vines of the canton. They set up roots in Swiss Romandie in Bole, a small village of the Neuchâtel *vignoble*, the wine-growing region. I'd like to go to this village someday to find out who this man was. My father never spoke to me about him. I told the mayor of the Berne district who allowed me to leaf through the chronicle and the old civil status registers of my native commune and who helped me to decode the graphic of family names, often irregular and fantastical: "Putting things in order is fine. But, tell me, do you not know among all these people whom I call my own, a single soul who strayed from the straight and narrow, who served time or mounted the scaffold? That would give me a hint as to where I come from."

CENDRARS: "No," responded the mayor to me, "except perhaps our most celebrated registrar, nicknamed "Talleyrand" by his contemporaries because he served faithfully under all the regimes, from Napoleon in 1851, up to the year he died, as a nonegenarian. The man was a night hawk, a drunk, a binger, a boozer who had a disruptive relationship with his wife, who also drank like a fish. He even served an eight day prison sentence for corrupt practices. Aside from this one failure to fulfil the tasks entrusted to him, there's no blemish on his record, and he's often held up as an example. Look at how his deeds are kept, and his spelling, his calligraphy. You couldn't do any better. He stuck his papers in an old cask taken from these Messieurs de Berne, during a brawl. He had a short fuse.

MANOLL: It was during your travels that you found the trace of your seven uncles?

CENDRARS: Yes, yes, yes, yes. But I knew more or less where to find them. They are my mother's brothers.

MANOLL: You spoke only of the seventh because he resembled you. And the others?

CENDRARS: The others? I have kept the others in my heart since my childhood. I was beside myself whenever *maman* received a letter from one of her brothers, these letters, as I put it in my poem:

> ...these letters with the fine exotic stamps
> which contained Rimbaud's verses in epigraph[67]

CENDRARS: One day, a notary of the family wanted to open one or two files for me concerning one of my uncles. If I had known about these documents earlier, *Le Panama* would not have been a skinny chapbook but a saga. My uncles all had destinies that were extraordinary, *hors-série*…

MANOLL: This story of the Panama, it's a poem you wrote under what circumstances, after how long of an incubation period? Was there still this ten year hiatus between the adventure you experienced and the moment that you wrote it down?

CENDRARS: A very long incubation. There's an entire subconscious, refinement phase that is necessary. Usually, I start with the title. I have a knack for creating good titles, that others tend to envy. I could cite a few and even among foreigners. "Listen, old pal," they begin, embarrassed, "I just finished such and such a thing, a play, and can't find a title, figure one out for me." Each time, it strikes me as implausible, but I find them a title. As for myself, once I have my title, I start daydreaming. Things start getting moved around. There's a conscious and unconscious crystallization around the title, and I don't write anything solid until I know all my characters, from the date of their birth to the date of their death, and I've had them develop under all sorts of circumstances possible and imaginable according to their character and their fictitious or real position. That can go on for years. I take notes. That's how I constitute files stuffed with notes and sketches. It's the imagination and not documentation. Documents get in the way for me. Take for example, General J.-A Suter, who was a historical character. I wrote *Gold* without digging inside the American archives and that's why I subtitled my story *The marvellous story of General J.A.Suter*. If I were to plunge into the Washington archives, an excellent repository of documents which could have been useful, I would have made a less synthetic book, much more historical, teeming with picturesque anecdotes and tailored to the life and times. For example, in one of the final editions of *Gold*, I added a small chapter because the script didn't yet contain any feminine lead or love interest, that I had intentionally left out with a view to a cinematographic adaptation of my work in America. The Companies with whom I was in discus-

.sion used editors and tekkies to dose and intercalate these scenes into films. I added a small chapter found in an old number of *Tour du monde*, year 1862, which cited the name of women gold diggers, some women who lived there, who went up to the Sacramento mine, and who handled themselves like men, fought with men, were of a fierce virtue. There were some Frenchwomen including one who was nicknamed Joan of Arc because one night she shot dead some Mexicans with a revolver. Another *Nini-Pantalon* because she didn't let herself be pushed around and boxed against men, even knocking out a few of them. A third, *Marie-get down now, girl!*, who smoked a pipe and exploited a highly productive placer deposit. She was given that nickname by derision because she was the wildest and terrorized the camps of the adventurers. She feared nobody. But where would I have ended up if I had taken into account all these documents! Besides, an original document that I had under the eyes, caused me to commit a monumental error which remains unforgivable since I knew the region of Sacramento, having hunted bear there. Imagine if I were able to bring the *bateau-mouches* up to *Place du Tertre* in Montmartre, what do you say, that'd be something monumental. Now, I am going to explain to you why I committed this famous blunder, that the American critics never failed to point out and that I have corrected since. I actually committed this monumental gaffe because I had under my eyes a document from the times, an original letter, written by old Martin Birmann,[68] the sole Balois who continued to correspond with Suter, the tutor of his children, his testamentary executor thereafter. In this letter, this fine man committed the topographical error in question and I was so happy to be able to give this moving letter, unique in its genre, a rare and precious document, that I lost all critical sense and I allowed myself to endorse this monstrous geographical error, but an error which proved to be very useful ten or fifteen years later when the Germans produced a film of my book, without authorisation and without having paid any royalties. Since I had the intention to sue them for five million in damages, Luis Trenker, the director and principal actor in the German film, distributed the film in Paris under the title "The Emperor of California" (whether rightly or wrongly, Luis Trenker today is adver-

CENDRARS SPEAKS

tised as being the author of the apocryphal *Memoirs of Eva Braun*, relating the tale of Hitler's wife). Trenker argued that the gold rush belonged to history: "General Suter doesn't belong to you," he argued, "the story of California doesn't belong to you; we don't know anything about your book." To which I responded: "If you don't know anything about my book, why did you make the same mistake in yours as I did in mine? Explain that one to me – the same geographical and topographical error that I corrected in a later edition of my book *Gold* that you are selling at the box office. I've had it recorded by bailiff." That put paid to his speech. But the trial never took place, because the Germans had arrived in Paris[69] and with it the occupation and the zeal that the Krauts brought to discrediting my work, at whatever the cost. Finally, they blacklisted me as a Jew. That had to be the low point! I was put on the "Otto" list.

MANOLL: Speaking of geographical errors, you referred to one committed by Victor Hugo in a poem…

CENDRARS: And that a Brazilian friend would frequently quote to me while roaring with laughter after we'd wind up a good lunch. He would wipe off his mouth while he emphatically recited this poem of Victor Hugo on Pernambouc where the great romantic praised Pernambouc and its blue mountain, whereas it's a flatland, and not a hill to be seen as far as the horizon.[70]

MANOLL: You found another etymology of Pernambouc…

CENDRARS: Indian, yes, in a Tupi dictionary, and another yet again, which provided me free of charge with the performance of a goat trying to desperately take to his heels in the foam as the sharks zeroed in on his neck…

MANOLL: As a matter of fact, I wanted to talk to you about that. So, you brought a goat on board to throw it to the sharks, which contradicts what you said one day about hunting tigers: "Do you think I am going to take out a magnificent beast barely out of bed, sitting on his butt, like a lovable puppy, scratching fleas from behind his ear, just because he's right in line of fire? I didn't come all this way to take out a drowsy beast coming out of a dead sleep. I hadn't come all that way to pick out my prey the way you buy a rug in a bazaar.

MANOLL: But you nevertheless did feed a goat to a shiver of sharks...

CENDRARS: I wanted to see how the sharks would react, and whether given their underdeveloped chins, they mightn't have to flip onto their backs to eat with their bellies exposed to the sun. Since the swill and white-water was already foaming, and my goat was fighting like hell to swim back to shore, I wasn't able to witness the shark feast, or even confirm that a shark feast had taken place. But, later, I had the luck to see sharks, in Uruguay, at the outfall of Bovril Co – the famous frozen beef producer. The sharks proliferate there. They gather by the thousands, splashing in a feeding frenzy in the bloodied waters flowing day and night out of the slaughterhouses, full of garbage and entrails. Monsters, with three rows of teeth – the shark they call the Whale shark has six thousand teeth in each of his jaws! – I was accompanied by the daughter of the director of the slaughterhouses, an Anglo-Uruguayan, the prettiest strain of South Americans, and we'd spend our time tickling the pilot-fish hovering at the left-side jaws of the sharks with long bamboo shoots. When we succeeded in dislodging one of them, you could see the imbecilic huge shark out of synch, disoriented by the loss of his navigator, hesitant, lost, having no idea what to do, breaking down into tears. You'd feel like getting down and hugging him, tickling him and pulling the stupefied beast out off the water, the beauty, if only he hadn't been so heavy. We were cracking up. Oh, did I ever have some fine days with this ardent young girl.

MANOLL: You also took a crack at hunting crocodile which I understand didn't turn out too well, I believe?

CENDRARS: You know, I don't really have the temperament of a hunter. Hunting actually horrifies me.

MANOLL: Wasn't it an old, really terrible crocodile?

CENDRARS: The life of animals is of great interest to me. I've shot films, documentaires on animals. So, when someone refers to a beast such as this "terrible" crocodile to which you are alluding, I'm always ready to go take a closer look. It was at the edge of a magnificent lake, in one of the most beautiful sites of Brazil. It seems that it was a massive Yacari Caiman, by his dimensions and by his age. But, I never saw him…

MANOLL: But you nevertheless nearly got killed by him!

CENDRARS: Oh! Don't exaggerate. I had my rifle with me. I jumped inside a skiff that was moored close by. The skiff was filled with water and there was an old box of soap floating on it. I grabbed the box to use as a scoop. Bad luck! It was filled with wild bees, thousands and thousands that swarmed onto me. I had long been warned about the stings of these bees, which are no bigger than a gnat or a midge, and insinuate themselves everywhere – into your nostrils, your throat, your ears. I was told "Copy the donkeys. When they are attacked by wild bees, they lie down and pretend they're dead." I dove into the water, thinking I'd escape the bees. Once I hit bottom, I suddenly recalled the croc, and climbed back onto the banks. I acted like an ass, all right, and lay down in the grass and played dead. After a few seconds, the bees left me alone. I've heard there have been mortal cases. The indigenous who watched me from afar crumpling with laughter. They won't forget me easily in the region, with my sad sack face and my useless rifle.[71]

MANOLL: What interpretation did you give – it wasn't a horoscope – to the prediction of this gypsy you went to consult, that is, that you were destined for a prison, voluntary prison.[72] What sense do you give to all that?

CENDRARS: A spiritual sense. It's from this voluntary prison that I have just escaped to return to Paris.

MANOLL: In fact, it's the prison of writing?

CENDRARS: I don't know. It's a spiritual prison. Besides, all the poets who are touched at a given time of their life by the rays of a certain star, the Shooting Star of Durer's *Melancolia* in his famous engraving, lapsing into a form of contemplation that can become an infinite and mortal despair which leads to suicide or folly as was the case with Gérard de Nerval, or yet succumb to extraordinary diseases and conditions that leave the physicians helpless and distraught. Just as contemplation can lead to the most sublime joys, as I believe happened with me. I'm not going to dwell on the point, because one shouldn't speak of these things. Touch wood. I am very superstitious.

MANOLL: You, Cendrars, superstitious?

CENDRARS: My dear friend, you cannot return from an experience in a virgin forest without coming back superstitious. The Indians are extraordinary people from a mental standpoint. They read your mind. There's no point in trying to spin lies or flatter them. They'll pierce through and expose you to the light. I attribute the failure of many expeditions which attempted to penetrate inside these mysterious and legendary cities in the depths of Amazonia or Mato Grosso, on the one hand, to the blockheaded mentality of the explorer – I cite from memory the ill fortune of Fawcett – and on the other hand, to this…how can I say this, to this faculty, to this gift of double vision that the Indians have.

MANOLL: That reminds me of something absolutely mysterious that you related. I am not sure whether we should take your strange tale for the literal truth. But you spoke of a magical plant that you said was called an ibadou.[73]

CENDRARS: Yes, the levitation plant. I believe that I am the sole white man to have ever culled a twig of it, yes, myself, yes.

MANOLL: And you tasted it to test its effects?

CENDRARS: You chew it like plug. No, I didn't taste it. I'm too horrified by drugs. In China, I never smoked opium, not even a small pipe out of curiosity.

MANOLL: You say there are plants that bark, that whistle.

CENDRARS: In the tropics, this phenomenon doesn't surprise anybody. On the *Côte d'Azur* you have the mimosa which is already sensitive, a plant which retracts when you touch it. The barking plant is a large-flowered orchid that the Indians cultivate on the tip of a rotten branch and that they suspend above the entrance to their straw huts. If you approach at a certain time of day, your shadow falling across this flower basking in the sun will be sufficient to cause it to retract and fold up, like the queen-of-the-night in our part of the world. It retracts while making a sound which is between the clacking of castanets and that of a dog barking, or like a hoot.

MANOLL: How did the Indians discover these mysterious plants and are they aware of the power that they possess?

CENDRARS: Tell me, Manoll, how did a Greek herdsman first have the idea to peel an artichoke to taste the inside, hidden beneath its prickly shell and how is it that a peasant from our land first began planting asparagus on the side to develop the tender stem and the pineal bud? In all the countries of the world, and during every era, the human species has been able to concentrate its mind on vegetals for the purpose of extracting food and poisons, an entire flora to cut which ranges from the gathering of mandragores and peyote to quinine, antipyretics and feculants. And who was the first man to produce the first grain? We have no idea. There are millions and millions of gramineals, and yet we still have no idea which botanist identified among all the wild herbs the mother herb which gave birth to wheat. And now, my friend, what is the question you wished to ask me from the outset, at the beginning of this interview. Have you forgotten it?

MANOLL: No, here it is: when you assert, Cendrars, that *I love life*, – and your entire work is nothing less than the illustration of this jubilation – do you mean by that to exclude what a certain literature claims to be the privilege of the creative mind?

CENDRARS: I think that there is a sort of errant monomania which pushes some towards the exploration of so-called unknown zones.

MANOLL: And the taste of Baudelaire to go to the bottom of the unknown to discover the novel, is that not similar to your going to the bottom of the known and the daily to find the novel?

CENDRARS: But, did Baudelaire not also confess: "While still a child, I felt in my heart two contradictory sentiments: the horror of life and the ecstacy of life"? From the spiritual, everything is novel for the person discovering the spiritual life. You can be born for the first time; you can be reborn for the tenth time within the same house, inside a house which is always the same and where one discovers the novel every time one goes off the beaten path. The writer who makes numerous u-turns during the course of his life, like me, never climbs by the same stairwell, never descends into the same cellar, and is never at the summit of the same tower. He unceasingly discovers the novel. Everything depends upon climate, the time, the moment, the humour, the inspiration, the sanctification, the exhaustion, the fatigue. O seasons, o castles![74]

CENDRARS: Allow me to compare this cry of Rimbaud to what Saint Teresa of Avila wrote in *The Interior Castle* on the return of the soul and its disillusion, its stagnation in the seventh dwelling after a charisma such as levitation or transport: "The soul which achieves the intimacy of the seventh dwelling place experiences almost no more of these impetuous ravishments. Even the states of ekstasis and flights of the mind become increasingly rare, and almost never occur in public, whereas earlier, they were very common occurrences." (I am citing from memory). On the other hand, I could cite for you, *The Dark Night of the Soul*, the beautiful spiritual canticle of Saint John of the Cross. But, I only know it in Spanish.

MANOLL: You have very, very frequently cited the aphorism of Schopenhauer: The world is my representation, which, is it not true, does not contradict, quite the contrary, this other phrase of disillusionment that we find in a good number of your books: "To write is perhaps to abdicate." What do you mean exactly by the term: to abdicate?

CENDRARS: Writing is not really living. In a nutshell, it's not life. To say it's the life of the mind, well, it's not the life of the mind. The life of the mind is contemplation. Writing is for us other writers, more and more, a way to earn cash, alas! And not the most amusing of all, nor the best paid, nor the most skilful. There are more rewarding ways to swindle people! So, it's a vice, or a bad habit; that's why it disgusts me ninety per cent of the time. I'm not the only writer who is saying that. It appears that Madame Colette also complains that she is obliged to write ceaselessly, and to go to such lengths to write well.

MANOLL: That's something else that you have often repeated. But in the end, if one considers the number of works that you have published, one sees that it amounts to a considerable number of volumes;

CENDRARS: There are about forty, maybe fifty, I don't know, but that is more product of my sloth than of my activity. I have never been a *Monsieur* who writes in my cabinet so many hours per day like a civil servant. These last few years, I've tried to make up for time lost during the occupation. *Eh bien*, at the end of the third, the fourth, the fifth volume – I think I wrote five – I was fed up, there was only one thing on my mind and that was bringing everything to a halt.

MANOLL: You have written a number of stories which are all "true tales", the last three books published, *l'Homme Foudroyé* (The Shattered Man), *Bourlinguer* (Vagabonding), *le Lotissement du Ciel* (The Subdivision of the Heavens)…

CENDRARS: The *Shattered Man, Vagabonding, The Subdivision of the Heavens, The Severed Hand*, there were four of them…

MANOLL: …these are books…

CENDRARS: That's more than enough. Particularly since people actually think I've found some kind of formula and that I'm going to keep using it to the bitter end. The editors themselves ask me to change nothing, but that bores me. I need to turn to something else now…

MANOLL: My dear Blaise Cendrars, it's now time to turn to the story of your life.

CENDRARS: Why? I don't see the point. I've already personally told everything I could say, and it's not finished, I still have other books in preparation.

MANOLL: Ah! You announce 33 volumes. Why 33?

CENDRARS: The list of 33 volumes that I announced for more than forty years is neither exclusive, nor with limitations, nor prohibitive. The number 33 is the key figure for activity, for life. So, it's not a black list. If it contains an index, it's not a blacklist. And it doesn't contain the titles of novels that I'll never write. The other day, I was surprised to discover *The Severed Hand*, a work that I only published in 1948, and which has appeared on this list since 1919. I had completely forgotten it! It also includes novels that I'm going to resume and that will be released over the coming years. Plus there are the ten volumes of *Our Daily Bread*[75] which are written but that I consigned in several bank safes during my peregrinations in South America. And, God willing, that will be discovered one day by chance. It's not signed and the deposit was made under a false name. There are also numerous poems to which I'm more attached than to the apple of my eye and that I can't bring myself to publish, neither by timidity, nor by pride, but by love...And then, there are the books which were written, ready for publication and that I burned to the despair of my editors, for example: *The Life and the Death of the Unknown Soldier* (5 volumes).[76] Finally, there are the bastards, the larvae and the inchoate fetal life-forms that will probably never survive onto the page. Which are they? How do you designate them? Far from recoiling in horror, when I lean into this interior teeming eddy, I draw upon force for new and different creations. 33 is the key figure of the creation, of life; an atomic pile. As a working title, and discounting the profits in advance, let's call the lot of them the Zoé pile: Zoé 33.[77]

MANOLL: I have to admit, you're an extraordinary workhorse!

CENDRARS: No. I'm an extraordinary daydreamer. I allow myself to drift into all my fantasies, even where it concerns writing.

MANOLL: We still have a few minutes. Would you like to recite one of your poems, for example, the beginning of the Transsibérien?

CENDRARS: Don't ever ask me that, Manoll. I have a horror of reciting poetry. It's bad enough citing others, but my own!

MANOLL: I'm sure you would give immense pleasure to our listeners...

CENDRARS: Don't push your luck. It's ridiculous...

MANOLL: But...

CENDRARS: All right, you go ahead and read the Transibérien; you have a fine voice. And get on with it, you still have around two minutes. It won't take too long...

Michel Manoll reads out a fragment of the *Transsibérien*:

In those days, I was still in adolescence
Barely sixteen years old, and my childhood memories erased;
16 000 km from the place of my birth
In Moscow, the city of a thousand and three clocktowers and seven
train stations
I couldn't drink enough of those thousand and three clocktowers
and those seven train stations
My youth was so sensual and so crazy
That my heart burned to the ground like the Temple of Ephesus
That my heart burned to the ground like Moscow's Red Square
As the sun fell beneath the horizon
My eyes would shine a beacon onto the ancient roads
I was still a bad poet
Who wouldn't die to the old life and pass Cape Bogador

The Kremlin was an immense Tartar cake
Encrusted with Gold
Gigantic almonds perched on bleached-white cathedrals
And the honey-gold of the bells
An old monk reading me the legend of Novgorod
My throat slaked with thirst
While I read the cuneiform codes
Suddenly, the pigeons of the Holy Spirit took wing on the square
And my hands took wing too, with the rustling of the albatross
These were my final reminiscences of the final day
Of that final voyage
And of the Sea.

Still, I was a bad poet
I wouldn't die to the old life
I was starving
And all the days and all the women in the cafés and all the drinks
I wanted to drink them all and pulverize them all
And all the showcase windows and all the streets
And all the houses and all the lives
And all the wheels of all the hackney cabs spinning like eddies
awash with scuttling cobblestone
I wanted to plunge them into a furnace of swords
I wanted to grind all their bones
And rip out all their tongues
And liquefy their drawn and quartered nude bodies under their
maddening clothes
I saw the coming of the great Crimson Christ of the Russian revolu-
tion
As the sun widened into an exposed gash
And became an inferno...[78]

VI

Al Jennings' Gun

MANOLL: You said in one of your poems, Blaise Cendrars, that Chagall...

CENDRARS: That was forty years ago, and it's been at least thirty-five since I've seen Chagall.[79]

MANOLL: He's one of your oldest friends.

CENDRARS: Friends tend to disappear from sight. Actually, friends just tend to disappear.

MANOLL: But you met him shortly after his arrival in Paris?

CENDRARS: In La Ruche,[80] which was an odd place.

MANOLL: Which Fernand Léger used to frequent.

CENDRARS: Who hasn't frequented La Ruche at one time or another? But I didn't meet Léger at La Ruche. We go back a lot further. Now, Chagall, he stayed there for a long time. Soutine lived there and so did Modigliani. A lot of people did. But, most of them were painters. As for the women, in the end, they're all *artistes*, aren't they?

MANOLL: You have told many tales about Modigliani.[81]

CENDRARS: Not so many, but someday I will get down to the task. I want to tell the world about his death and his funeral. It's a grisly story but typical for Montparnasse Bohemia. You could even say it drove the last nail into the coffin of the *Montparnos*. Since that point in time, they are an extinct line.

MANOLL: You spoke about his character.

CENDRARS: I spoke of his notorious drunkenness. I drank a lot with Modigliani. We went on some mind-reeling binges. When I think about it, it strikes fear into me. How did I manage to come out of it with my mind and health in order?

MANOLL: You recounted a highly amusing story about Modigliani attempting to walk on water next to the *Square du Vert-Galant*. Apparently, he got it into his head that he could walk across the south arm of the Seine and plant a kiss or two on the washerwomen he'd spotted toiling on their riverboat *bateau lavoirs** on the left bank. That was during the war. Was that during one of your leaves?

CENDRARS: No, no, no, no. It was after the war of 14, and we were both very miserable. But I had known Modigliani since his arrival in Paris. He was rich. He was living in the Hôtel du Perron, *rue du Dôme*, and I was living with my mother on *avenue Victor Hugo*. The Modigliani I knew had just arrived from Livorno in possession of his father's inheritance. He must have had around two hundred-and-sixty-thousand francs at the time. He was a very elegant young man with a small hand-sewn jacket, cut off at the hips, narrow, clinging, with sleeves that fell precisely to the wrists in the style favoured by Italian tailors. The Italians know just how to do to allow

---

* boat wash-sheds

the cuffs of the sleeve to bubble out, thus giving maximum effect when you gesticulate. I can assure you that when I met him, Modigliani was rich. Very rich.

MANOLL: Didn't he have the habit of reciting the Divine Comedy to anybody crossing his path? Had he learned it by heart?

CENDRARS: Dante and quite a few other things. Modigliani arrived from Italy with a social painting style, just like Van Dongen arrived from Holland with a proletarian style of painting – painting for the State if you like. The evolution of émigré painters after landing in Paris is a highly amusing and unpredictable phenomenon to observe. I saw Modigliani much later with Fernand Léger.

MANOLL: Was this at the time that you published *La Fin du Monde* (End of the World) with the colour illustrations of Fernand Léger at **Editions de la Sirène**?

CENDRARS: Actually it was well prior to the war, when Fernand resided on the *rue de l'Ancienne Comédie*.[82] We'd meet up every day for an *apéro* at the corner of the *rue de Buci*, alongside the pimps, the girls, all the tender and coarse riff-raff of the quarter. We used to knock back *vin blanc au citron*, a tomato, a *môminette*, which is a Pastis straight up. Absinthe cost five sous, the *môminette* three.

MANOLL: Was that by any chance the Cinq-Coins?

CENDRARS: A bistro, the headquarters of the newspaper hawkers, just like a bit further up, the Trois-Portes was where the old guard of the Mercure de France used to scrum down – Dumur, Meurice, Van Bever…

MANOLL: Léautaud…

CENDRARS: No, not Léautaud. Léautaud was *chez le boucher*. We'd see him pass by in his velvety Levite cloak, made of luster.

MANOLL: Wait a minute; the *Cinq coins*, that reminds me of something…but what?

CENDRARS: One of my elastic poems..and I'm sure you won't mind me reading off a bit…it's just a little poem composed while in a state of advanced alcoholic intoxication. Alcoholic intoxication and poetic intoxication. The two go together very well…this won't take long.

At the five corners

Dare for once and shatter the silence
Everything is colour, movement, explosion, light
Life blossoms on the windowpanes of the sun
And melts in my mouth
And I'm free-falling, translucid onto the street

I heard you say it, old man

I can't open my eyes?
No need with a golden mouth
The world of poetry hangs by a tether.[83]

MANOLL: And who were some of the painters you saw in those days?

CENDRARS: We saw them all. Paris has never been short of painters. Nor has Montparnasse. Montmartre even less so. Painters by the truckload, almost as many as today. Although they seem to be multiplying exponentially today…

MANOLL: True.

CENDRARS: …If you judge by the number of exhibitions, galeries, boutiques selling paintings and what with inviting the press to gala evenings, paying them all cocktails, and whatever. The art vendors, Bernheim, Hessel, Paul Guillaume, the Rosenberg brothers, none of the lot interested me with the exception of Ambroise Vollard.[84]

MANOLL: He was a close friend.

CENDRARS: A great friend. A grand friend.

MANOLL: Well, that's why I'd like you to set the record straight. A lot of people take pleasure in defaming Vollard.

CENDRARS: Come now, Parisians have been defaming each other since time immemorial. If your project is to set the record straight…

MANOLL: He's a man who was scurrilously smeared by some.

CENDRARS: Scurrilously. Especially by the painters who were most beholden to him and finally found the courage to slander his good name after he died.

MANOLL: Yes, certain painters who are best left unnamed. But the truth isn't there. You who are one of the closest friends of Vollard…

CENDRARS: I may have mentioned him two or three times in my books.

MANOLL: He spoke of you in his Memoirs, in particular about the purchase of a house which he constructed in Tremblay.

CENDRARS: At Tremblay-sur-Mauldre. I'm the one who convinced him to buy that house, the house of the Templar. The mason of the region wanted to have it demolished to have a stone quarry in the centre of the village and save money for the cartage transport. He was a gentleman, who had several building complexes and a splendid garden. During his lifetime, Vollard lodged Georges Rouault there, and then Picasso.

MANOLL: You lived at Tremblay.

CENDRARS: Yes, of course I lived there. That's where I wrote *Gold*.

MANOLL: It was while on his way to see you that he had a blackout.

CENDRARS: He was killed in an auto accident. Smashed his head against a telegraph pole, at a bend where he lost control of his vehicle, just prior to arriving at the Sainte-Apolline crossing.

MANOLL: Did you know a Gitan named Sawo?[85] That's an amusing tale. Did you penetrate the gypsy world then?

CENDRARS: He was one of my pals in the Legion. His uncle ran an itinerant theatre.

MANOLL: An itinerant theatre?

CENDRARS: Yes, during the winter he'd park out in a vacant lot in Gentilly. During the summer he worked the fairs. But Sawo no longer formed part of the caravan. He was a lad who had taken his distance from his own people, a black sheep.

MANOLL: It's through him that you managed to become part of this insular community?

CENDRARS: For Sawo, there was nothing picturesque at all about their community. He had emancipated himself and had escaped them.

MANOLL: So, it was while tracking down Sawo that you managed to penetrate the clan?

CENDRARS: No. I met him by chance in Paris. His hangout was a place called the Critérion, just opposite the Gare St Lazare. That's where he served his apprenticeship as a gangster. The Critérion was frequented by fraudsters, counterfeiters, the quack jewellers and the pawners, the English fences, and other dealers in stolen jewels.

MANOLL: You've related numerous interesting anecdotes about the customs of the Tziganes. Especially about the matriarchy.

CENDRARS: Nobody really knows anything about Tzigane customs. It's very difficult to figure them out. People spew out rubbish about things they know nothing about. Even the specialists who have looked into the matter haven't really shed any light on the issue. They spin hypotheses. Nobody has made any progress, not even an inch. The enigma remains entirely unresolved. Just recently I received a long letter from a Tzigane tinsmith who wrote: "You either lied in your book or the fellow who was with you took you for a ride. There's not a true word in anything you wrote about us."

MANOLL: Did you follow up on that?

CENDRARS: Why would I? I wrote my story. I published it. And the little Tzigane was behind me."

MANOLL: What are your sources then?

CENDRARS: How I lived with them. That's what I recounted. They told me this and that, and then I told the story of what they told me in my own way. The little tinsmith who wrote me probably came from another clan, maybe even another race than my Gitanos. You see, they come from the four corners of the planet. So, of course, the little tinsmith called me a liar. Why wouldn't he? He's from Montreuil, they're all *Romanis* out that way. I defer to his jurisdiction. We corresponded for a while. Finally, he confessed that he wanted to get into movies. I got him a job with Jean Faurez, the director, who wanted to shoot a film on the life of the Gypsies. We'll see whether that goes anywhere. Faurez had already hired Carmen Amaya, and that didn't work out; She didn't want to compromise herself by doing a tzigane story, because she was a tzigane.

MANOLL: You spoke about the matriarchy and the role of the husband.

CENDRARS: What I recounted was accurate as far as the people I knew were concerned. Those I knew travelled in caravans. Gitans in the caravans that I came across were the caravans with whom my people fought. No doubt they call me a traitor, a dirty lying scumbag, a *pacha*…

MANOLL: That's very funny.

CENDRARS: What do you find funny in that? Think about it. If I wrote about the customs of the firemen of the city of Paris, their brothers from the city of Tours would say I'm exaggerating and none of it's true…

MANOLL: Of course they would. Did you follow them and did you stay for a long time with them?

CENDRARS: For the New York people, it's something else again.

MANOLL: You frequented the Gitans of New York?

CENDRARS: Who said anything about New York Gitanos? I was talking about firemen. In the Americas, there are a lot of Gitanos, particularly in Brazil, because the Gitanos were the secret bankers of the kings of Portugal. When they were expelled as Moors and sent into exile abroad – they were the ones in the end who financed them, jointly with the "new Christians", the label for converted Jews who had abjured to escape with their lives and who also went into exile on board ships for which they had secured armament for the discovery and the conquest of Brazil. They had been conferred privileges – horse breeding, taming and dressage and the prospection of mines, gold, silver, diamonds, emeralds, while the native Lusitanians who expatriated had difficulty in procuring concessions if they weren't to the manor born. Already, during the colonial era, the Gitanos of Brazil were rich. In spite of that, they conserved their traditional mores and even today, the clan is as much a secret society as it ever was.

MANOLL: Sounds pretty mixed up, all these stories about the Gitanes.

CENDRARS: It's horribly complicated. I would argue that they originate from the Canary Islands, that they are ancient Guanches. I'm sure I'm not the only person who holds this opinion. Dr Capistan, the Director of the Museum, a man who spent his entire life studying the civilisation of the Guanches, the last Atlantis, was almost convinced of it. Gobineau thought they came from the Indias. I wouldn't know.

MANOLL: In this book you're promoting, *La Carissima*, are there any stories about Gitanes?

CENDRARS: Not at all, it's got nothing to do with them. I already told you that La Carissima is the novel of St Mary Magdalene, the most beautiful love story ever, about the greatest love that has ever existed on this planet.

MANOLL: You followed their ways; you lived with the tribe of Sawo for three months?

CENDRARS: Which led me to Méréville,[86] the capital of the watercress beds.

MANOLL: Where you used to draw salt from water cressons.

CENDRARS: Yes, yes, yes, yes, yes!

MANOLL: A pharmacist once said he made a fortune doing that.

CENDRARS: And with a lot of other things, which didn't prevent him ending up in Auschwitz, poor fellow…

MANOLL: Were you in a difficult situation?

CENDRARS: The children of this poor Israelite, it's ghastly…

MANOLL: What did they eventually become?

CENDRARS: I don't know. Probably they ended up following their father into the ovens…

MANOLL: You haven't had any word or information about them?

CENDRARS: How could I? My own sons were prisoners in Germany. A bloody mess. A fiasco!…

MANOLL: Couldn't you have helped them?

CENDRARS: I've helped all kinds of people in my life. But there's a fatal twist. You end up losing sight of each other. Sometimes I meet somebody whom I only see once, and who I'll never see again, and then I forget him. And that even occurs with good friends, like this pharmacist and his family. If I had to recall all the people who I've met in my tumultuous life, I'd be travelling around with a battalion. No, such a thing is impossible. And, besides, to each his own destiny.

MANOLL: How did you get the idea of extracting salt from water cresson?

CENDRARS: I found some water cresson, I extracted salt from the water cresson, and then I sold the formula.

MANOLL: You had all the right tools?

CENDRARS: Don't forget. I'm the son of an inventor.

MANOLL: And you also pursued studies in medicine.

CENDRARS: Sooner or later, I was going to end up doing something like this.

MANOLL: These studies, you abandoned them and then resumed at a later date?

CENDRARS: Oh! I abandoned them a long time before the war. I actually think I left off with studying at the right time since humanity is becoming more and more robotic. *Eh bien*! Doctors are becoming like garage mechanics. They don't speak in tongues anymore; they prefer universal tongs. Rather than crack you over the head with a crowbar, they use a wrench to tighten up or loosen screws. Just take a look at pharmacies today. There's nothing but specialists anymore. There's no more pleasure in being a pharmacist, in knowing the old-fashioned hidden remedies and recipes and having a knack for things. Somebody asks you for some indecipherable remedy that he insists is amazing, and then rings off some long-winded chemical equation – there you see? Another specialist – and then starts shuffling around muttering to himself, now which drawer is it in, which shelf did we stick it on, this filthy concoction, and under what number? So, you consult an alphabetical index. Coucou, are you getting the picture?

MANOLL: You stayed in Méréville country for a year. That is where you wrote a book for Mr Doucet, the *couturier*, a book which is called *l'Eubage* (the Druid).

CENDRARS: It's a miniscule book, of little worth.

MANOLL: How did you come up with the title?

CENDRARS: By thumbing through the Petit Larousse, a book I couldn't live without!

MANOLL: I think you said the *Eubage* was a Gallic priest.

CENDRARS: Yes, according to the Petit Larousse, a Gaulois priest who studied natural sciences, astronomy, divination.

MANOLL: It's a book larded with scientific plates, reproductions, photographs.

CENDRARS: Well, in that form, it was never released. It was never published in the way that I had conceived it and today, all this documentation is a bit out-of-date. Nothing becomes obsolete faster than scientific documents. The original manuscript is in the *Bibliothèque Sainte-Geneviève* and can be consulted. I delivered it one chapter at a time to Mr Doucet.[87]

MANOLL: How did you come into contact with Doucet?

CENDRARS: I have no idea. One fine morning, his servant came knocking at my door to ask on behalf of Mr Jacques Doucet whether I would consider writing a book for him. I didn't know anybody named Jacques Doucet and I told him so. Later, we became great friends. He frequently invited me to lunch. We dined very well in his home. We drank some fine bottles together. He treated me well. He would invite beautiful women, theater actresses, the most elegant of his clients. He was an elegant man, and with me he was utterly charming.

MANOLL: In a word, he was a patron of the arts.

CENDRARS: Much more than a patron of the arts. He had a razor-sharp wit. he had *esprit*. One day, he described Cocteau in a manner that I'll not easily forget. Jean was coming to meet him in Switzerland, at the *Right-Palace*, dressed up as a butterfly collector, with the net, the plant collection box slung across the shoulder, edelweiss on the ribbon of his tyrolian cap, alpenstock, serrated shirt, leather shorts cut off at the knee, Scottish socks, large hobnailed boots, descending fresh and pink-cheeked from the Paris express. An obsolete engraving of fashion. Cocteau had brought a copy of *The Frivolous Prince* for Doucet, which he had signed and dedicated.

MANOLL: He was a seasoned collector.

CENDRARS: He was an extraordinary collector! But, much more than his collections, it was his excentric, manic way of collecting that interested me. So, he'd collect paintings, but actually he created much more work for the frame-makers than for the painters. He ordered frames from them in extravagant or unexpected volumes or demanded precious materials. As a result, the frames ended up costing him a lot more than canvasses of the modern masters. Was it irony or was it an attempt to shame the painters for their lack of imagination? Curious man. One day he told me that his favourite game as a child was to rummage about with a fishing rod in the sewers under the *rue de la Paix* where he'd hunt rats. This naturally

scandalized passersby, men and women alike, who were utterly re-
pulsed and horrified by the odour of stirred-up sewage emanating
from him. Consider it if you will, Mallon. *Monsieur* Doucet, the
Duke of elegance and the couturier of kings and the courts of Aus-
tria, Russia and England, training to be a sewerman!

MANOLL: Didn't he place orders with every writer of your generation?

CENDRARS: With everybody. And not only from our generation
but also with the previous one –Suarèz, Valéry, etc. They wrote on
demand for years and years for Mr Doucet. Finally they were beaten
by the surrealists who monopolized Doucet right up to his death.

MANOLL: And all that was bequeathed to the *Bibliothèque Sainte-
Geneviève*?

CENDRARS: That's right. Go ask Miss Marie Dormoy who is conservator of the Doucet collection. She can confirm.

MANOLL: So, was it around that time that you went to Brussels and
to London in a music hall?

CENDRARS: In Brussels, I couldn't count the number of times I
went, so what are you talking about? In 1909, I was appearing as a
bit player in the *Théâtre de la Monnaie*. I first played in Carmen,
for 3 sous per night. At the 1910 World Exhibition, I was selling
rugs, loukoum and peanuts in a stand, disguised as a Tunisian.

MANOLL: And what about the music hall in London, when was
that?

CENDRARS: Oh that was a long time earlier!

MANOLL: And how about movies, the cinema. That came a lot later?

CENDRARS: What?

MANOLL: When did you first become interested in movies, and in
making movies?

CENDRARS: I wanted to make movies, and as luck had it, I had the
opportunity to work in England. I shot several films for an English

company who for currency exchange reasons, sent me off to Italy. I stayed for nearly a year in Rome making movies, up until the time of the march on Rome and the triumphal entry of Mussolini. Before that, I had already worked with Abel Gance. Even earlier, I had shot documentaries for Pathé, short documentaries, and one series: *La Nature chez elle* (Nature at home with itself). I wrote scenarios, synopses (as they're called), dialogues, did some cutting etc.

MANOLL: Earlier, when I was talking to you about that, I wanted to bring up your meeting with Charlie Chaplin.

CENDRARS: Charlot? I never did any movies with him. He was a clown in a music-hall.

MANOLL: I know that.

CENDRARS: I was a juggler. I still had both my hands at that time. But I'll tell you something even more extraordinary. Lucien Dra, the first publisher of the surrealists, *Place de la Trinité*, was world champion of diabolo and was performing in the same London music-hall. Do you have any idea what diabolo is? It's a sort of double spinning top or reel that you cause to roll on a tight string between two sticks that you shake from left to right and from top to bottom to give the top a rotating and accelerating movement prior to launching it in one *élan*, very high in the air. Then you catch it back on the string held tight when the aerial top falls back towards the ground. Then you repeat the cycle until exhaustion and relaunch it endlessly, higher and higher into the air. Lucien Kra had circled the globe as the diabolo champion. He had perfected his spinning top, one roared, one opened up in mid-air, at the nadir and rained out a shower of small flags, a third exploded into a shower of sparkles. His success was prodigious.

MANOLL: Henri III had his bilboquet.

CENDRARS: You couldn't have put it better. The diabolo is really just a modernised bilboquet. But did you know that the bilboquet is as old as the world itself and is a national game in Africa? You can find different models in Livingstone's *Voyage to Zambezi*, and engravings showing Negroes playing bilboquet in the presence of village chiefs and a large audience – probably a contest of sorts. In Brazil, they use the "devil's bilboquet" in certain conjuration ceremonies. It's a magical bilboquet, the 18th century model, but I'm not sure why the Brazilian Blacks call it the "bilboquet". Is it a simple difficulty of pronunciation or does it also form part of the ceremonial of sorcerers casting curses and spells? The name has such an importance in magic and the two "l" that are added to this name are possibly devils horns!…

MANOLL: So, you had no idea what Charlie Chaplin would become one day?

CENDRARS: Neither did Charlot. Neither did Lucien Kra. Neither did I. Charlot had no idea he would one day be the greatest comedian in the world. Lucien Kra didn't have a clue he'd one day be a specialist in the avant-garde poetry of Paris. And I didn't know I'd be the author of the Transiberian. One shouldn't swear on anything. These are things that one can neither divine nor foretell.

MANOLL: During the war, despite the military rules that strictly prohibited it formally, you took a lot of photographs. I presume that today they are now lost. In the lot, there was one…

CENDRARS: I had a small Kodak. I had a lot of troubles because I was shooting photos on the front. Somebody stole my camera at Surgery post 53 in Champagne. The surgeons purloined my arm while the nurses picked my pockets. In the end…I'm not complaining; All that is a long time ago.

MANOLL: I wanted to talk to you about a photo.

CENDRARS: What photo?

MANOLL: The one published in *Le Miroir* in 1915. The photo which shows your comrade Bikoff, a soldier of the Legion who had disguised himself as a tree. When you saw the film, *Shoulder Arms*, you said to yourself that Charlie Chaplin had used this photo.

CENDRARS: For sure. To shoot his film, *Shoulder Arms*, Charlot had to do documentary research on the war by consulting countless illustrated sources, including *Le Miroir*, where the photo of Bikoff appeared.[88] And it's this same photo which must have given him the idea to camouflage himself as a tree to entrap and emprison Wilhelm II. It was his best film.

MANOLL: Didn't you have the opportunity to meet Charlie Chaplin when you were doing some reporting in Hollywood?

CENDRARS: When I was in Hollywood in 1936, Charlot had just finished doing *Modern Times*. He didn't want to receive me because in his own words: "...Before the premiere of my film, I feel like I'm on the electric chair, and after the première, the current keeps tickling me in the epigastrium..." He was in such a nervous state that I didn't insist.

MANOLL: What sort of relations did you have with him when you were together in the London music-hall.

CENDRARS: No relationship.

MANOLL: He was just a little clown?

CENDRARS: A clown among a hundred other clowns.

MANOLL: You worked for awhile in the same club, then you lost sight of each other.

CENDRARS: Listen, I did what...eight days, fifteen days in London.

MANOLL: You didn't keep in touch.

CENDRARS: We didn't.

MANOLL: Not at all?

CENDRARS: Since I had reinvented myself as a juggler, I juggled and when years later, I had my right arm amputated and I found myself in the hospital, eh bien! I started juggling again with my left hand to regain a sense of balance and ease of movement, and I got so good at it, that what had first started out as a con and something of a pastime and then became my bread and butter, eventually became my greatest moral support at the Lakanal lyceum in Bourg-la-Reine where I was cared for.

MANOLL: And Al Jennings, you met him in Hollywood?

CENDRARS: Yes, I met him in Hollywood.

MANOLL: …the terror of Oklahoma. Didn't you translate one of his books?

CENDRARS: A formidable book no matter how you look at it. He is the sole person to recount the life of O Henry in prison, a great man, for whom I have a great affection. He's the most popular of American authors, a man who American men of letters scorn because he only wrote in short story reviews. As if contemporary US men of letters would have any quibbles about writing in their grand de luxe format magazines! You have to wonder what grounds they have to reproach a convict who didn't have any choice in the matter, other than the fact that he had single-handedly conquered New York solely by force of his talent. He's the inventor of this genre that is so difficult to master, because the only way to manage the trick is to be able to combine great art with great probity, and even more importantly, a great heart which is sensitive to joy, to the unhappiness of the popular classes, and doubled with a spirit which is impulsive and malicious: *the novella in 1000 words.* Not one more, not one less. He published ten, twelve volumes of them. A master. I doff my hat to the man.

MANOLL: And Al Jennings, the train robber?

CENDRARS: When I met him, he was seventy years old. He was a decrepit, wizened old man, no higher than a boot, extremely agitated, excessively sympathic, with limpid eyes, the look of a child, a magnificent innocence and red hair. When I asked him to show me how he handled his revolvers in all these famous battles where he had stood his ground against the sheriffs of the Far West, the odds a hundred-to-one against, he planted himself on his spread-out legs, stuck his two fists on his hips, pulled out two 47s which he aimed at me, rubbing his belly, balancing lightly from one foot to the other, to lengthen or widen his shooting range, so he could quasi-automatically spray an entire zone, "like with a modern machine gun" he said. He was superb. Prior to taking leave of each other, we drank a whisky of course, and as a souvenir of our meeting, Al Jennings gave me one of his revolvers. I was pretty choked up. And so was he, I believe.

MANOLL: Is that the first time an outlaw gave you his weapon?

CENDRARS: There were others. There was the prisoner of Tiradentes, in Brazil, then that stationmaster who I told you about earlier and who gave me his assassin's knife, a long pernamboucaine blade, long as a machete as a souvenir of my visit to his prison. But Al Jennings! ...I'm telling you friend, when a man of that vintage hands you his weapon, and trusts you with it, it's no wonder I was choked up with emotion.

VII

Joseph Stalin and *Gold*

MANOLL: While leafing through the letters of Max Jacob[89] this afternoon, my dear Blaise Cendrars, I came across a page that concerns Modigliani and which fortunately adds to what you have already said about this character. Would you have any objection to me reading it?

CENDRARS: No, go ahead. But I find the coincidence curious. Imagine that I just happened to cut out for you from the most recent number of *Nouvelles littéraires* which publishes it, a letter addressed to the painter Picart Le Doux and where Max gives him news from Montparnasse. I brought you the cut-out so you could get a glimpse of just how Max can shake up the coconut palm. You haven't seen it? Good, I'll read out the letter after you read yours.

MANOLL: After you, *cher ami.*

CENDRARS: No, I'll have none of it; you go first. Read your letter.

MANOLL: Here is what he said about Modigliani: "…He was impoverished. He came to me to borrow three sous for the metro to take him to Montparnasse. Because I didn't have it, I borrowed the money from madame Lafleur, the concierge. Picasso, our neighbour said that only Modigliani knew how to dress himself. I believe that he was the first person to wear blue-and-white chequered ticking shirts. He said it was all the fashion in Italy. He always carried his copy of Dante with him. He could infuse the verses of Dante with such life, and play their harmony with such dexterity that it seemed that it was he who had composed them. Modigliani was a small enough man, with curly hair. He had a flat, but handsome profile, and a pale face that was fairly round. His laugh was clipped but seemed to burst out, bitter and yet childlike. He was stiff, all of a piece, violent in unexpected ways, due to his appearance of gentleness, sentimental despite his rigidity and his indignations, sardonic more in appearance than in reality. He was solely an artist and a poet. He was obsessed with art. Gallant, and an Italian madrigal with women, capable of sudden cruelty. He loved courtesy, but didn't overdo it. A true gentleman…"

CENDRARS: That's good, that. He was a bon vivant and a real skirt chaser. I always saw him with women of all categories and all types, but they were all beautiful, very beautiful. Now, I am going to read you the other letter of Max. You will see how he treated young poets. This letter dates from 1916: "…*In Montparnasse new poets! Cendrars, reformed soldier, shaking the stump of his arm he was so drunk. In his verse, he imitates well the folly of Rimbaud and fights with Reverdy. He is a southerner, shooting off his mouth or remaining silent, very diplomatic. No culture? He's found a monotonous chord that resonates in his verse and in prose. He is the poet of The Flip side of Heaven, with reverberations and top hats and always the house empty, the cellar, all that delicate and gloomy. Like my small poems in prose, but sadder. – Paul Dermée, professorial or at least could be mistaken as such, studies our methods, started by a conference on*

*me, very gay in society, the gaiety of the Sorbonne, a bit noisy and
mocking. Reads a lot, does translations, has all the honest means of
eking out an existence, the inside of his house was nicely appointed
with marble wall panelling. He likes to invite his friends to dinner.
The Pilgrims of Emmaus on his wall. His wife is Romanian and discreet. He'll go far. A bit of Socrates and a bit of Don Quixote with a
pince-nez and a lottery ball ogle – Apollinaire's sojourn to the front
has calmed him down: he never forgets his standing as an officer. On
that topic, he is reminiscent of the priests who taught him his lessons
during his early childhood. – Picasso will return from Rome with the
décors of a Russian Ballet…– Alice Derain has just left my home, she
is penniless: but I'm saving my money for the printer. – Courage, pa-
tience. Pray to God just as I try to do: it'll bring you joy…"* Eh bien,
my dear Manoll, I think you have been well served, you who didn't
want to believe me!

MANOLL: Max Jacob, as a person, did you know him well?

CENDRARS: A bit.

MANOLL: Did you see each other at the *Soirées de Paris*?

CENDRARS: No. I used to drop by and see him on *rue Gabrielle*,
when I was wandering around Montmartre, or I'd cross his path
when he dropped by Montparnasse selling his books in cafés: he
always had a bundle under his arm: *Saint Matorel, La Côte* (Breton
songs), *The Allies are in Armenia, The Dice Cup, Le Phanérogame,
the Cinematoma*, that I edited at La Sirène. He sold all these books
to the highest bidder as a street hawker.

MANOLL: There's another character to whom you've yet to refer –
Arthur Cravan, the poet, who claimed he was the nephew of Oscar
Wilde.

CENDRARS: Sorry to differ. On the contrary, I am the only person
to have spoken about him, in "The Sidereal Eiffel Tower".[90] He was
a poet and a boxer, and actually, he was a nephew of Oscar Wilde,
on the maternal side. He liked to sign his manifestoes: *Arthur Cravan, the poet with the shortest hair in the world.* But he honoured
himself with all sorts of other titles as well, each of them more sug-

gestive than the previous: burglar, taxi-driver in Berlin, giant orange picker in the California orchards, blackmailer, etc. etc. He was really a precursor of Dada and the sole disciple of Jarry.

MANOLL: He, Robert Delaunay and you formed a trio that didn't go unnoticed at the *bal Bullier*, and who stood out like sore thumbs. Wasn't one of your trademarks an extravagant, gaudy cravate?

CENDRARS: As a boxer, Arthur Cravan was the strongest, the heaviest and the huskiest of the three of us and he knew all the male tricks of the trade and all the tricks of a henchman, but he was a yellow-bellied coward, despite all his posturing and bluster. Since he'd called Guillaume Apollinaire a Jew, the two poets were to fight in a duel, but since Guillaume no more desired to affront this hulk of a man on the ground and Arthur wasn't any more eager to put his physique at risk, which he required to parade around and bully people and pump up his chest in front of women, the two men cooled off, and jointly agreed that each of them would record their version of the event, and this naturally received no little publicity at the time. Since Guillaume Apollinaire proved that he was not a Jew, but Roman Catholic, Arthur Cravan declared: "I have no difficulty in acknowledging that the Jew Apollinaire is not Jewish, but Roman Catholic." This nonsense, which Apollinaire declared himself satisfied with, and that the two poets signed, appeared in Cravan's review: *Maintenant*. Apollinaire's two witnesses also signed. To compensate for his failure to produce witnesses, Arthur followed his signature with all sorts of fantastical titles: there was a full column of them! And the incident was declared forclosed à la Père Ubu…

MANOLL: Didn't you wear gaudy, extravagant cravates?

CENDRARS: Sure, loud, gaudy American ties, made for showing off.

MANOLL: And Cravan, didn't he have a rather curious way of dressing?

CENDRARS: Dark-coloured shirts, even black, twenty years prior to the fascists. What we called "the dirty shirts" after the bloody Monte Falcone affair. It's curious this role of colour of shirts in the inter-war period: brown in Germany, blue in Spain, green in Brazil, gold in Mexico.

MANOLL: Did Cravan wear the tails of his shirt outside his trousers?

CENDRARS: He allowed his shirt-tails to hang out behind and to lead people to believe that these tails were in fact actually turds of excrement, prior to going to the *Bal Bullier*,[91] he would squat on Delaunay's palette, which would cause Robert to flush with indignation, because at that time, Delaunay was using a lot of lapis-lazuli in his blues, which was costing him a fortune.

MANOLL: Didn't Gino Severini, the delegate of Marinetti in Paris, telephone the Futurist Centre of Milan to describe your costume?

CENDRARS: Severini or somebody else, a great beanpole whose name escapes me, but who I had a fistfight with one night at the Stock Exchange just in front of the telegraph wicket. He was telegraphing about our dress code generally, but more particularly, and with precision the details of the dress of Madam Sonia Delaunay, *la robe simultanée*.[92] It was a real communications agency. Milan was broadcasting the news of these events throughout the world as Futurist demonstrations, and did such a good job of it that our acts and gestures and our harlequin outfits from the *Bal Bullier* (I believe Delaunay wore a multi-coloured tuxedo one night!) were celebrated and emulated by an avant-garde that slavishly adopted what they now perceived to be Paris' latest fashion. But our extravagances particularly influenced the Moscow futurists, where we were seen as the trend-setters.

MANOLL: In those days, didn't Mayakovsky wear lemon-yellow shirts?

CENDRARS: That's what I heard. But, that wasn't new in Russia where everybody wears his shirt-tails over the trousers and where the satinet shirts are in pretty well every colour of the rainbow.

MANOLL: You said that you envy Mayakovsky having a neon newspaper on Red square in Moscow.[93]

CENDRARS: What can I say? I don't know any other poet in the world who has such luck and the opportunity to use a neon journal to publish or more precisely to display his poems in the street.

MANOLL: But, it's nothing more than a marketing stunt!

CENDRARS: I don't believe so. It's not marketing.

MANOLL: Well then; it's propaganda!

CENDRARS: I don't think so. It wasn't propaganda. Coming from someone else, sure, maybe so, but coming from him? Mayakovsky had too much love for his people and for poetry! That wasn't the problem. Think of the millions of illiterates in Russia. It took nothing less than the genius of Mayakovsky to animate this crowd. And that's where I envy Mayakovsky. His poems weren't spoken. His poems weren't written. His poems were drawn. Drawing is comprehensible, even for illiterates. It wasn't obscure or enigmatic and what audacity and what invention! The only man comparable is Walt Disney, who is also a beautiful inventor, although less pure, and the greatest poet of the United States, even though he's industrial. I am convinced that today Mayakovsky would spew out his poems on Red Square by loudspeaker and that he would improvise every night by radio broadcast to find listeners at the ends of the earth, creating newer and newer poems, revolutionary in form and in spirit.

MANOLL: You also spoke with great admiration of the anonymous aviator who traced CITROEN in gigantic letters in the sky of Paris. You even described it as poetry and the aviator didn't know himself that he was creating poetry.

CENDRARS: As ephemeral poetry, it was marvellous, not to mention being a feat of acrobatic prowess of quasi-insurmountable difficulty in the sky and in high winds. He had to reverse his trajectory to accurately place the trema on the E of the name CITROËN and not in some slap-dash approximate way. He flew upside down so as to better execute the stunt.

MANOLL: Of course, not an easy thing to get right.

CENDRARS: He spewed out two dots of smoke over that "E."

MANOLL: Speaking of Cravan, you also said that his talent was immense, but my generation is completely unaware of that. The works of Cravan are nowhere to be found.

CENDRARS: I wanted to publish this at *La Sirène*, but in those days, the death of Cravan was not a certainty and I had to abandon the project. Anyways, he didn't publish much outside of two or three long poems in his review *Maintenant*, extremely rare but which can be found in the Jacques Ducet collection at Sainte-Geneviève.

MANOLL: Did you attend the famous conference in a codpiece?

CENDRARS: Of course, since I was the one who first told the story.

MANOLL: The carafe of water was replaced by a bottle of absinthe and he announced that he would down the entire bottle in a single shot.

CENDRARS: He also announced that he would show up wearing a codpiece to find his true love, and then he came, clothed in impeccable, flannel trousers. Once again, he lost his stomach for the fight.

MANOLL: You once told a story of Arthur Cravan in New York...

CENDRARS: Because it was in New York that he made his true débuts and became a hit due to his style, his need to please and simultaneously create scandals. His sojourn there wasn't long, but his influence endured.

MANOLL: Who did he meet there?

CENDRARS: Marcel Duchamp, a high-strung, deadpan professor of chess and French gallantry, a boy with much talent as a painter and who had exhibited the series of *Nudes descending a stairwell at high speed* at the 1911 show of the Independents, which had a massive influence on the pre-war futurists and more recently on abstract painters.

MANOLL: Isn't he the one who said that a toilet is a work of art?

CENDRARS: Of course, and quite a few other paradoxes, and well prior to Dali! Anyways, he doesn't paint anymore, which today is irrefutable proof of his intelligence. I adore this boy. He amuses me.

He's no dupe.

MANOLL: And Picabia?

CENDRARS: Having left New York to seek treatment for his shingles case in Switzerland, then meeting Tzara in Zurich where Tzara was a refugee, Picabia then initiated him in…

MANOLL: Cravanism!…

CENDRARS: If you like and if you mean by that a mountain giving birth to a mouse: Dada…Dada is Dada and Arthur Cravan is its prophet!…

MANOLL: And how did Cravan die?

CENDRARS: He was murdered in a boxing academy he opened in Mexico City. A stab of a cutter into the heart. We don't know why, or by whom nor for what motive. Probably something to do with a woman, a bird.

MANOLL: You have said that the letters that Arthur Cravan sent from Mexico to his wife in Paris contain marvels.

CENDRARS: The ones I have read are pure masterpieces. Cravan must have suffered a terrible spiritual crisis under the influence of the climate and the tropical nature of the environment which caused him to feel abandoned and lost in the savagery of God. He had travelled to the South to prospect silver mines, as he wrote to his wife he had done two or three times. Cravan was impatient to return home a rich man after the war, and upon contact with this ancient Mexican people, foreign Indians on Planet Earth, closed off, hostile to contemporary life, nostalgic, blood-thirsty. I compare his letters, filled with adoration and cries of revolt, with Novalis' *Hymns to the Night* and Rimbaud's *Illuminations*, which is rather astonishing for anyone who knew Arthur Cravan, his sloth, his volatile humours, his elephantine physique. But, I repeat, nothing is certain. He must have been afflicted by something.

MANOLL: The other day, to switch topics, we spoke of *Gold*…

CENDRARS: I think I have said everything I have to say on the topic…

MANOLL: I think there are still some things to say on the topic. It's a book that has had an extraordinary destiny. It has been translated into twelve languages…

CENDRARS: I know of at least two dozen translations, including one in Japanese.

MANOLL: And even an edition in Braille for the blind.

CENDRARS: And a school edition in Holland which is used as a French language manual in the colleges of this country.

MANOLL: What is even more interesting is that it fell into the hands of Stalin. Is that true?

CENDRARS: There was an American engineer, I.D. Littlepage[94] who the Soviets had hired to develop the gold extraction industry in their country, or rather, to create a profitable concern to extract gold in Siberia, to the North of the Love River, in the region of Kolyma, who said that Stalin's bedside reading was *Gold*. It's possible. *Gold* was published in 1926 in Russia, in a translation by Victor Serge.[95]

MANOLL: Do you think that it was *Gold* that gave Stalin the idea to start prospecting gold veins inside his own country?

CENDRARS: I wouldn't give too much credence to that one.

MANOLL: But, don't you think that it could have given him that exact idea?

CENDRARS: I think it could have given him the idea, but that doesn't mean it did. According to Littlepage, it gave him the idea. Other testimonies insist on this point.

MANOLL: Generally, the press only presents one side of Blaise Cendrars. They speak of a brawler, a daredevil, an adventurer, when in fact, by your own admission, you are a contemplative…

CENDRARS: Yes, and that's another form of adventure!

MANOLL: Furthermore, this evidence is easy to establish, because it already abundantly appears in your own work. You have recounted how in your childhood you read Saint John of the Cross in Castilian, later St Thomas Aquinas and Saint Teresa of Avila, later again books on demonology, magic and certain chapbooks of Raymond Lulle, for whom you published *Le Livre de l'Ami et de l'Aimé* [The Book of Friendship and Love] at La Sirène, translated by Max Jacob. On this famous route N10 that you described so many times· in your South American stories, route which you evoked so many times in certain South-American tales, a road that for you led to the ends of Brazil, or even in Paraguay, you brought Migne's *Patrology* with you in the car…

CENDRARS: You don't really think that I lugged along my four hundred in 4 volumes inside my vehicle? To commemorate a certain chapter of my life, every year I purchase a tome of the *Patrology*. It's true that I've been doing that for thirty-five years. But I only bring one copy with me no matter where I go and as baggage, this single volume is often very cumbersome…

MANOLL: A certain chapter of your life, you say; are you referring to your meeting…

CENDRARS: A certain chapter of your life is what I said. That's nobody's business!

MANOLL: Besides, we already have a reader's insight where you have expressed your sorrow over the burning of the Alexandrian library, the disappearance of the *Tora Nueve*, the Tower of Books of Mexico.

CENDRARS: We don't know much about this disappearance, except for the fact that the Spanish, and particularly fanatical monks threw something like 230,000 Mexican papyruses into their bonfires as works of the Devil.

MANOLL: You are solely interested in desperate people, in children, in the disabled. I'm thinking of all your true tales, including the tales, the reportages and the translations. For example, Suter, the hero of *Gold* is a "desperado". Al Jennings,[96] the train robber, is another. Bringolf, the bigamist, is a third. Al Capone also. You translated his *Memoirs* in a collection that is called "The Desperadoes").[97]

Are there others?

CENDRARS: No, there are only two volumes in that collection: Bringolf and Al Capone. But I had prepared twenty and there could have been two hundred. The topic is inexhaustible!

MANOLL: Did you meet Al Capone?

CENDRARS: Yes, I met him.

MANOLL: In Chicago?

CENDRARS: In Chicago.

MANOLL: In Miami as well?

CENDRARS: No, in Chicago.

MANOLL: It was during the time when he was considered the gangster patriarch of Chicago?

CENDRARS: I knew him when he was the beer baron. Chicago gangsters were waging the beer wars. It was the height of Prohibition.

MANOLL: The mafia was involved in a lot more than brewing beer.

CENDRARS: Americans only drink beer and whisky. Don't waste your time hawking wine in that part of the world. It was only about ten years later that the bad boys of Marseilles opened a speakeasy in New York where you could drink wine, if you knew the password to get in. For a Frenchman like me, those Marseilles boys saved me.

MANOLL: Among your heroes, I recall the sexton of the cathedral in the cathedral of Santiago of Chili. Did you ever meet him?

CENDRARS: No, I was told the story by a group of Chilean women. He died about twenty years ago. I don't even know his name. For me, he's like one of these anonymous saints.[98] He still hasn't been canonized. It's not my problem. It's not like I have to intervene in the matter. All I know about the matter is that they're looking at beatification in Rome.

MANOLL: He performed some extraordinary feats.

CENDRARS: What he performed are miracles. His parish priest couldn't handle it. He formally prohibited him from continuing. He was scared out of his wits that the local bishop or even Rome might get involved. A while after that, the sexton of Santiago spotted a worker carrying out repairs on one of the cathedral towers, when suddenly he fell. "Ohé!" he shouted at the worker who was free-falling to earth at 32 per square. "Stop, hold on right there!" which brought the worker's fall to a halt in mid-air. "I have to find the curé to get permission to perform a miracle! Back in a jiffy!"

CENDRARS: Luckily, when he returned, with the curé breathlessly running behind him, the worker was still suspended in mid-air, between heaven and earth, head down and his arms spread-eagled. "C'mon down, old man, take it easy, nice and easy, nothing to fear. The curé says it's okay if I work a miracle, it's all on the up-and-up!" With that, he gestured him right towards him and welcomed him inside the folds of his coat.

MANOLL: Really? Tell me, is there a cult devoted to him in Chili?

CENDRARS: No, not yet, but give it time. There's a grand devotion. A grand popular feeling. People gather around his tomb. Apparently, they bring the ailing to his graveside.

MANOLL: I have no doubt about it. I wonder, were you thinking about him when you wrote the story about St Joseph of Cupertino?[99]

CENDRARS: What are you talking about? There's nothing even remotely similar between the two. Saint Joseph is the champion of levitation.

MANOLL: Well, sure, but the sexton of Santiago of Chili, he knew a thing or two about levitating too, right?

CENDRARS: Nah, he didn't really fly himself, not really. He never flew. He never received the gift. You see, the gift, how can I put it, is like a charisma. You have to have the charisma. Now, Saint Joseph of Cupertino, he'd get dragged upwards, and then he'd be carried upwards. He wasn't even aware of it. It was like a visitation. Grace entered him and he'd start flying without any help. One day, he even started flying backwards. I can tell you the other Brothers in doing their Matins or vespers in St Francis of Assisi chapel were totally stupefied, while he's flying around right over their heads. This first performance of aerial acrobatics was during 1645. And I'll tell you, right up until Sunday, 18 December 1949, he held the record. The sole aviator to have flown backwards. Then, go figure, I receive a letter during late December 1949 from a friend. While doing some gliding he gets caught in a mistral squall, and he couldn't straighten out his flying machine, so he had to fly backwards all the way to Cuers-Pierrefeu. Now, figure, he left from Saint-Auban-sur-Durance, that's ninety-six kilometers flying backwards! Saint Joseph's record was broken.* (BC Postscriptum 1952: Since the newspapers reported this feat in December 1949, I have no scruples in mentioning the name of the French aviator who broke the record of Saint Joseph de Cupertino flying backwards. It was Charles Birod, an old glider pilot, a complete Ace).

MANOLL: Are you the first to discover the acrobatics of Saint Joseph of Cupertino?

CENDRARS: You're joking, no? Voltaire referred to him, but it was solely to deride him.[100]

MANOLL: Are you the one who made him the first patron saint of aviation?

CENDRARS: You're obviously still joking. I don't have to turn Saint Joseph into the first patron saint of aviation since aviation already has other patrons. Anyways, I don't know how one appoints someone patron saint of aviation. I even wonder whether it's the aviators who choose their patron saint, or whether it's the patron saint who chooses the aviators.

MANOLL: Isn't there a medal in America for aviators, struck with the effigy of the saint?

CENDRARS: I heard about this medal in the American press, but I've never seen it. I have interviewed numerous American aviators. Most of them were not aware of it, others had heard of it, but they didn't wear the medal. I don't know whether it's a decoration or a badge.

MANOLL: Blaise Cendrars, I haven't forgotten that you have taken an interest in aviation since its beginnings. You have told the story of the creation and development of an aircraft.[101]

CENDRARS: The Borel aircraft, a triplane, the ancestor of the Goliath. The first cargo plane. I worked on the propeller.

MANOLL: As you related in *Moravagine*, you worked on the development of the aircraft. How did that come about, in passing?

CENDRARS: Why wouldn't I? I like mathematics and the curves of a propeller, its profile, its angles of attack are amusing to calculate.

MANOLL: Did you fly?

CENDRARS: Everybody flew in those times. The mechanics, the lab personnel. We spent most of our time busting up our wooden contraptions.

MANOLL: What is extraordinary in *Moravagine* is that you had already predicted the crossing of the Pacific.

CENDRARS: Yes, I had conceived *Moravagine* as a sequel to *Fantomas*, an adventure novel.[102]

MANOLL: But you gave an exact itinerary of the crossing. How was such a thing possible?

CENDRARS: I'm not sure what itinerary you're referring to. I had studied the question. The day when aviators would choose to finally cross the Pacific, they pretty well had to choose the same approximate itinerary that I had charted out.

MANOLL: You not only predicted the crossing of the Pacific, but also that of the Atlantic.

CENDRARS: And why not around the world? I have already reserved my seat for the first trip to the moon. Alas! It's not for tomorrow morning.

MANOLL: You knew Saint-Exupéry[103] who is already a legendary character.

CENDRARS: Saint-Ex? I met him in Paris. I never met him in the air.

MANOLL: When you were in Rio de Janeiro, you saw his plane passing on a daily basis. You even said that everybody set their clock in Rio around the passage of the French plane. That's how punctual Saint-Exupéry was.

CENDRARS: People thought it was him, but it wasn't the sole plane of the Aéropostale, where Saint-Ex was pilot. As for the writer, I met him once in Les Deux Magots, one other time with Gide, a third time at Lipp, and a fourth time when we were shooting *Courrier Sud* at Paramount studios. He seemed happy that day. He had just pocketed a thick wad of banknotes. So, he was bursting with good humour. And I liked the way he laughed. "Look at him," said his wife, Consuelo, who not only went by a nickname à la George Sand, but who was a character right out of George Sand. The grandmother of Nohant loved Consuelo who smoked cigars. "Look at him! He's a big child!" It's not like Sinclair Lewis who I never saw so pathetic as that day when I put him on the train in Rome, to go collect his Nobel Prize. He wouldn't even buy me a drink, and the night previous I had just saved his life! It is true that he was severely hungover that morning and that probably he didn't want to drink, or he'd taken a vow never to drink again. But, you know, the oaths of a drunk are always honoured in the breach!"...

MANOLL: What exactly are you saying?

CENDRARS: As unlikely as it might appear, it's a true story. It was around 1930. For some time already rumours about the author of *Babbit* were circulating in Italy, where he tramped about with a squadron of wild New York girls who were creating a scandal. One fine day, he disembarked in Rome, where I was shooting films, and told me that he wanted to meet me on an urgent basis. I told him to come see me in the studio, but he said he couldn't be bothered, that he didn't like movies, and that moreover, he didn't have time to come, as he was leaving the next morning for Stockholm to collect the Nobel Prize. I didn't have the time to disrupt my schedule either, as I was overburdened with work. But, that same evening, after a power outage at the studio, around 10 pm, I went to his hotel, where I fell onto half a dozen beanpole Americans, already completely in their cups, who were in the process of confecting a gigantic cocktail in a soup vat filled with whipping cream. They were pouring while squabbling with each other about something to do with the dose, two or three litres of vermouth. I couldn't find it in me to join in the antics of these wild women who were beckoning me to come and cut their hair. I was executing a u-turn in front of the one trying to pass me the scissors, when I hesitated and started to scope out the apartment for the incumbent resident master of the house whom I had yet to detect. The door of the bathroom was ajar. There was a flush of steam. I entered. The bath was overflowing, and both the hot and cold water faucets were turned up to maximum. Two dress shoes varnished, hung outside the bathtub. Stretched out in the bottom, a man in a tuxedo was in the process of drowning. I got him out of his fix. That's how I saved his life and how the following morning, he managed to take the train for Stockholm to collect his prize! It's no surprise that he looked so sombre. He had a hangover, a migraine and a bump on his forehead. Anyways, Sinclair Lewis wasn't handsome or even amusing to frequent. I have photos of him that would frighten the wits out of you. He was probably possessed, and he certainly wasn't happy. I have only known one other writer to put on such a face, like a necrophagic mask, a face haunted by terror, filled with wrinkles and folds, the Vaudois Ramus[104] who I never saw smile, even when he was tippling a glass...A strange drama...

VIII

The Death of Sarah Bernhardt

MANOLL: My dear Blaise Cendrars, you used to trap armadillos!

CENDRARS: The armadillo is a small and very amiable animal, and easy as hell to trap.

MANOLL: You, uhh, grab him by the tail, is that right?

CENDRARS: The armadillo is a noctambulist. He's very fearful. At the slightest sound, he rolls up into a ball inside his shell. As an extra precaution, at dawn, he digs a hole inside an embankment and slides into it, but he doesn't bury his tail. You sneak up on him and you grab him by the tail, stick your finger up his rump, he seizes up, panics, and retracts, pulls in his claws that he usually uses to grip onto the walls of his burrow, starts shaking, let's himself go. Then you pull him towards you, stick him on a skewer, set a fire of boughs and twigs and you use his carapace as a bowl, and you eat him. Very tasty. The flesh is tastier than rabbit and as white as a grain-fed range chicken.[105]

MANOLL: That reminds me of the menus that you cite in your poems[106] – extravagant menus, such as shark fins pickled in brine. Did you choose them to provide some local colour or did you actually try them, these local menus?

CENDRARS: Of course I savour them, these delectable menus. You could publish an entire book of those kind of menus. The other day, I was on *rue Bonaparte*, leafing through a book translated from the Chinese on Chinese cuisine. The recipes listed, the mode of cooking, the spices, and the sauces were making my mouth water, because, to tell the truth of the matter, I was starving to death in Peking…

MANOLL: Do you actually like Chinese food?

CENDRARS: I only know Chinese cuisine and French cuisine. Outside of French and Chinese cuisine, there aren't really any national cuisines, except maybe among the cannibals.

MANOLL: What was your favourite food in China?

CENDRARS: I don't know. In Peking, I ate in vile greasy spoons. Most of the time, I ate standing up at deep-fry stands out in the gusting wind. I only had enough to buy stuffed donuts cooked in rancid oil with a bowl of rice. On good days, it was fish rice or pork rice. I wasn't exactly on speaking terms with the mandarins…But in Paris, with a Mandarin friend in a grand Chinese restaurant, *rue du Colisée*, I ate lacquered Peking duck and crispy ginger beef. It wasn't all that great, but my host wolfed it down. The duck came from China, tightly wrapped up in strips of very crusty seaweed and sewn into wild rhubarb leaves and it reeked, which proves that the Chinese don't like preserves and don't use refrigerators, as they far prefer hanging their poultry.

MANOLL: Have you tried bird's nest?

CENDRARS: The last time I had bird's nest was at the home of my publisher, Mme Jean Voiler,[107] with Pierre Benoit and Roland Dorgelès. Pierre Benoit mirthlessly laughing, while Roland vigorously protested. He said he preferred a sea-salt beef stew! I found it a little on the brackish side, but to be honest, it wasn't bad.

MANOLL: What is it exactly?

CENDRARS: It's a mollusc baptised with the name because of its form. It's fished out of the Red Sea. It's the orange-footed sea cucumber, an echinoderm. It's still a dish for the wealthy, reserved for the old mandarins. Apparently, it's an aphrodisiac.

MANOLL: Among all these adventures that you have recounted, and that happened to you on *route nationale* 10, you have also spoken of the angels of the tomb of Dona Inès, in the Church of Alcabaça, Portugal.

CENDRARS: Yes, it's the tomb of Inès de Castro, the lover of Don Pierre the Cruel, the protagonists of the greatest love tragedy of Portuguese history: A supreme romantic tale which served as inspiration for Montherlant's play after an entire series of Portuguese and foreign writers, novelists and playwrights, differentiating particularly, I believe, the tragedy of Luis Veles de Guevara: *Reynar después de morir* (To Reign after Death). When Inès de Castro, who was the mistress of the *Infante*, bore him a son, the Court hatched a plot to strangle him. Driven mad with rage and pain, the prince swore he would wreak exemplary and unbridled vengeance as soon as he mounted the throne. Upon his coronation as king, Don Pedro o Cru kept his promise and on the very day he swore his oath, he massacred the three principal assassins of his lover. Then he exhumed the deceased, transported her solemnly to the Coimbre, installed her on the throne, smothered her with caresses, crowned her and Don Pedro proclaimed her the Queen of Portugal, swearing on the Gospels that Dona Inès was his legitimate wife. By a gesture of refined, exquisite cruelty, he forced all the nobles and the grand minions of the realm who participated in the conspiracy against Inès de Castro, men and women, regardless of their rank or the grandeur of their house, to attend and kiss the hand of the dead queen and to publicly seek her pardon. Montherlant, of course, shuddered at this grandiose and macabre scene. I wonder why? It's a pathetic scene. The tomb of Dona Inès à Alcabaça is a masterpiece of Bourguignon sculpture and the six angels that surrounded the recumbent figure – three men, three women are, according to a tradition, the portraits, men, of the assassins, the women, of three grand dames of the aristocracy who were the principal conspirators in this tragic intrigue. Thus, the revenge of Don Pedro was complete and the cruelest blame of all was reserved for the public humiliation inflicted upon the ladies of the Court.

MANOLL: You still speak of the pilgrimage of Santiago de la Compostella. Have you undertaken it many times?

CENDRARS: I have never gone on the *camino*, but Compostella is a place where I intend to travel soon with a friend. We have been talking about it for years, but we're having trouble reaching agreement because I want to carry out the pilgrimage on foot, the only proper way to do it, and by following one of the most ancient itineraries coming from France. My friend's wife, although a very good hiker, is hesitant because of the children. I advised using one or two donkeys to cross Spain, but I absolutely refuse to do this pilgrimage in a vehicle. That is why we have yet to depart on the camino.

MANOLL: What is the haunted chamber of Sarauz that you have spoken of?

CENDRARS: It's a blue bedroom, on the second floor of a beautiful castle. The portrait of a countess of times gone by hangs on the wall. During the night, on certain dates of the lunar calendar, the countess descends from the frame of her canvas and stands out on the balcony. Having learned that, I asked whether I could stay the night in the haunted chamber, but the countess did not appear.

MANOLL: Where is Zarauz?

CENDRARS: It is thirty or forty kilometres south of Saint-Sebastien, in one of the most romantic sites I have ever known. A *conche* [marble basin], fifty terraces, a hundred thousand rose bushes…

MANOLL: Didn't you cross these borders around the time of the Spanish revolution? You found yourself suddenly in the presence of a car of the Anarchist Federation?

CENDRARS: Yes, a car of the P.O.U.M. (Partido Orero de Unifacacion Marxista).

MANOLL: How could you cross these borders around the time of the revolution?

CENDRARS: There are no borders for a journalist.

MANOLL: You first came across this car of the anarchist Federation and then, you ran into a car of the Phalange?

CENDRARS: I selected the zone where I was driving because it was controlled by pretty well nobody, and I wouldn't fall across more than a single car of the Phalangists; It just so happened that I was passing through in the night and we ran across each other. Everything went quite smoothly. I'd printed out about a hundred business cards, BLAISE CENDRARS, War correspondent…civilian! I gave them French cigarettes, and in exchange they gave me some cigars from the Canary Islands, *puros*. With the P.O.U.M. men, we traded news of events. Each encounter lasted about five minutes.

MANOLL: And your escape in Saint-Bertrand-des-Comminges?

CENDRARS: In Saint-Bertrand-de Comminges, the venture remains so confidential that I can't elaborate.

MANOLL: Well, you spoke about it in "Rhapsodies gitanes".

CENDRARS: I know. I haven't forgotten anything.

MANOLL: Nevertheless, I'd like to put a question to you, even more indiscreet, by quoting the first dedication of "Rhapsodies gitanes", which reads as follows:

To the countess of Castries

in memory
of Calaoutça
of Casa Sedano
of 102, rue de Grenelle
of Saint-Bernard de Comminges
of the dinner of the Basque Farm
of the blind Abbot
of the Historical Minotaur – of the Blessed Crocodile
of poor Groumand dead in Geneva
and not to forget the Son of the municipal Sergeant
and the Man covered with women
THESE MEDIANOCHES
with my tender and long-winded friendship
B.C.[108]

MANOLL: All that could be the subject matter of an entire interview...

CENDRARS: Intentionally, I appended to each of my dedications a contrived mask confectioned from transparent plastic material which deforms them so they cannot be identified, but the interested parties had no trouble recognizing themselves, just as I wanted it. So, I'm not about to tell you who that is now.

MANOLL: And, who is the blind Abbot?

CENDRARS: Guess!...I didn't go to all this trouble to draft enigmatic, yet perfectly transparent clues so the first neophyte on the scene could mock me and spread gossip.

MANOLL: So, that will always remain an enigma for the reader.

CENDRARS: And what bloody difference should that make to me, if you don't mind me asking?

MANOLL: This first dedication is a curio item. And there is another...

CENDRARS: Fortunately. There are four in all. Surely you're not going to cross-examine me on all of them?

MANOLL: In "Rhapsodies Gitanes", dedicated to the infant Eulalie, you say that you played knucklebones with her. How, under what circumstances did you make her acquaintance?

CENDRARS: I know my word and the malice and spite of people, my dear Manoll, so I'm not going to expand any further. That might amuse people who muse aloud as to whether Cendrars isn't a braggart and must surely be exaggerating! I am very proud of my dedications and I went to great lengths to draft them in plain words to be sure that I could blur the traces of the enigma. One day will come when the scholars will be in the fray trying to elucidate these texts just as for centuries; they have been trying to decode the quatrain of Nostradamus. These divinatory quatrains were written in a magnificent language which has given me great joy, but they remain indecipherable. I have been reading them for forty years. I gargle with them. I wallow in orgasmic ecstasy, but I cannot understand them. I have never sought the key. I have read almost all the published keys, they are beyond reckoning and they are all false since every two, three years a new set of keys is invented without managing to unlock the enigma; but, as a great French poet, Nostradamus is one of the greatest. Yet another who I'll stick into my *Anthologie de la poésie française* if I ever compose that.[109] All these twists and turns of a conventional language invented impromptu beats by a longshot the DADA zaniness and the automatistic writing of the surrealists and the decalcomania of Apollinaire's *Calligrammes.*

MANOLL: I give up. I surrender. I won't ask any more questions about your dedications. These matters are far too personal for you to reveal.

CENDRARS: Couldn't agree more.

MANOLL: But I will put another indiscreet question to you: tell me, are you still writing to Manolo Secca?[110]

CENDRARS: I wrote to him recently.

MANOLL: I should explain who he is: a gas jockey who owns the most remote gas station in the Brazilian outback.

CENDRARS: At an interim terminus of a road which one day will end in Bauru, on the Rio Arana, unless the virgin forest swallows it up in the meantime. It's a savage region.

MANOLL: Hasn't he carved out a strange Stations of the Cross?

CENDRARS: A prodigious Stations of the Cross. At the time, about twenty-two or twenty-three years ago already, it was already comprised of half a dozen chapels. The arrest of Christ in the Garden of Gethsemane, for example, included sixty-two characters, Roman soldiers, the apostle Peter drawing his sword, the other, the one with the sliced ear, the Jewish ringleaders…, etc. On the way out, I stopped off to fill up with gas, but on the return trip, I stayed for eight days, plunged inside an oil drum to get rid of vermin: ticks, lice, the chigoes, eggs, larvae, which you pick up in the bush, from the interior jungle, the swamps from the ocean of herbs that crawl and swarm under your skin. So, I had the time to see how Manoo Secca ran his shop and to chat a bit with him. He was cutting down trees out in the forest, selecting the mahogany barrels that he worked in the glade prior to hauling them and putting them in place nearby the pump. Once the statues were ready, he would bring them to life by painting them in the same manner as the old Portuguese masters, in a flesh colour, *incarnar*. When I was there, he was in the process of gilding the armours of the Roman legionnaires.

MANOLL: Aren't they all installed inside automobiles?

CENDRARS: They're all inside autos. Whenever I write him, I send prospectuses of automobile brands, preferably coloured brochures, giving the most recent models, to serve as inspiration. Since Manolo doesn't know how to write, he never responded to me. I don't know if he's still in the world, or if the Secca gas station still exists. But I write from time to time to this upright and grandiose man, lost in the solitary depths, and will keep on writing to him as long as the post office doesn't return my sendings with the usual stamp: "Moved no forward address"! But you never know in those countries, and Manolo Secca was already very old…

MANOLL: Do you remember how he represented Pontius Pilate?

CENDRARS: Washing his hands in the sea, and not in a basin. It's his only character who isn't inside a vehicle. Since Manolo Secca fought in the Cuban war, and returned with a wooden leg, he represented Pontius Pilate as an admiral, standing up, at the fore of an American battleship and with arms so long that he could dip his hands into the Caribbean sea from the ship. He was a Black Spaniard. I don't know how he ended up shipwrecked in the depths of the Brazilian jungle. He's a saint.

MANOLL: Do you know that he kept his promise to do a life-sized sculpture of you sitting in the driver's seat of your automobile?

CENDRARS: Ah, that! He surely must have done that. I also sent him my photo.

MANOLL: You don't have photographs of all that? The Brazilian papers didn't publish anything? Is he known over there?

CENDRARS: He is absolutely unknown. The newspapers have never spoken of him. As for the photos that I developed, they were lost during the pillage of my cottage in Seine-et-Oise.

MANOLL: Nobody ever saw these Stations of the Cross? No other traveller…

CENDRARS: There are barely three passersby in a year…

MANOLL: That's a shame.

CENDRARS: It's a shame, and it's a benediction for him.

MANOLL: I hope that one day you'll receive a photograph of this statue which claims to represent you.

CENDRARS: I doubt it. The Brazilians aren't a curious people. They adore their country, no doubt about that, but they're complete layabouts. They don't really like the idea of tourism. As a matter of fact, automobile tourism doesn't even exist yet in the country. I inaugurated a number of unpaved roads where motor vehicles had never passed prior to me. More than one of these roads or byways ended up retaken by the bush and the forest. Last I heard, they were being replaced by asphalt roads. But isn't it a bit late to start on that?

The future is with planes.

MANOLL: I'd now like to discuss the coal sack, this mysterious thing…

CENDRARS: I can't precisely tell you whether the coal sack is a constellation of the Brazilian sky. It's exactly the opposite of a constellation. It's more like an immense hole, a stain so black in the sky, just under the Cross of the South, that people call it the coal sack.

MANOLL: I haven't forgotten that during this trip, you related in "The Sidereal Eiffel Tower" that you visited the cabinet of Doctor Oswaldo Padroso, a planter who was in love with Sarah Bernhardt.[111]

CENDRARS: He was love-sick.

MANOLL: I am asking you this question because I know you had the good fortune to meet Sarah Bernhardt during the final years of her life.

CENDRARS: Ill fortune is closer to the truth, because I witnessed a distressing tragedy during the final week of his life, that couldn't have lasted several years. An American director, whose name I don't even recall, tracked me down so I could give him a hand. He had made a contract with Sarah, but she was dying. So, she was costing him a fortune and this man wanted to get some bang for his buck before she died. Since he couldn't speak a word of French, he wanted me in a supporting role to gain some time and ensure that the film was produced. No time to lose. This man literally wore her out.

MANOLL: She was drugged like a racehorse.

CENDRARS: It was a pathetic, distressing spectacle.

MANOLL: You saw her die?

CENDRARS: Yes, yes, yes, and for an idiotic film, the name of which I've entirely forgotten, a piece of ineptitude without a name.[112] It was shot in the Chat Noir. Sarah had a role as a witch, a card reader, of god knows what. She was disguised with a pointed *turlututu* on her head, a white wig, a parrot on the shoulder, a magic wand, or a telescope in the hand, I can no longer recall, and it was so garish, a crescent moon behind, stars in front of her...

MANOLL: She had her wooden leg then?

CENDRARS: Of course, she'd already been amputated ten years earlier! Everything was filmed in her apartment in Villiers. The shoot had to take place there due to the time constraints. "Hurry, hurry! Time is money..." the American was shouting. Naturally that honey-eyed voice of hers wasn't recorded. It was still the silent film era. It was so absurd, criminal...I don't even know if the film was released...

MANOLL: When you were on assignment in Hollywood,[113] did you visit the Walt Disney studios?

CENDRARS: Of course, in fact it was the only studio that interested me. I was impatient to see how so much poetry could come off the assembly line. Walt is an extremely gifted young man. His production is very poetic and the most refined of the twentieth century.[114] He hasn't yet been examined under this light. His cartoons are pure poetry. Although they come off the assembly line, there's virtually no compromise on quality. I have already said a word or two on Mayakovsky. Which gallery will finally do an exhibition of Walt Disney's cartoons? It is high time that we take a closer look of the successive deformations of the drawings of Donald, the duck, the dog, or to borrow from Picasso, of the bull. We'll see which of them has gone the furthest in terms of comic invention, endearment or that special humour particular to Walt Disney. But one thing that is even more amusing than the Walt Disney factory is a *Negro Ball* that took place every Monday. Black chamber maids working for the biggest Hollywood stars who came to dance and drink. It often ended up in fistfights. In the rags of their bosses. I often witnessed groups of blacks who were the biggest names on the silver screen mimicking their antics, because Monday was the day-off for domestics.

MANOLL: You still haven't mentioned these two thousand writers under contract in the studios.

CENDRARS: It's an extraordinary chapter in the universal history of literature. But, there's too many of them…

MANOLL: Do they work as bureaucrats, punching the clock every morning?

CENDRARS: They are required to be there every morning at the same time, and they actually have to punch their timecards like other studio employees. In America, they're very strict about attendance in the workplace.

MANOLL: What do they actually do?

CENDRARS: They have to keep really busy doing nothing. The ultimate key for a writer under contract, if he doesn't want to lose his place, is to never collaborate on a film.

MANOLL: But the scripts are surely written by somebody?

CENDRARS: That's the enduring mystery about the studios. The ideas are somewhere in the exosphere. Somebody captures them and they're digested, ground up, outlined, chewed to pieces, revised, reshot, re-sketched, complicated, merged and finally typed out black-on-white on the machine by poor shmucks who aren't even hired by the studio. The writers under contract, who form part of the staff of firms, outsource the work to these people. Nobody really knows how, but the script always somehow ends up on the table during meetings – there's one of those per week – and God forbid that you should actually take the floor, or even express the slightest opinion pro or contra. Do that and you're out. They'd far prefer to pay severance than take the advice of a writer under contract. The writer is a shit-disturber. If eventually the film goes to production, nobody really knows who has the final say among firm management, the producer, the sponsors, the stars' agents, the representatives of the studios, the press, the marketing people, the censors, the feminist leagues, etc. It's a labyrinth.

MANOLL: And the pay is lucrative?

CENDRARS: Astronomical. You can make millions, and it comes in for years.

MANOLL: A name?

CENDRARS: Vicky Baum, among two thousand others!

MANOLL: You met Thomson, the masseur of the stars. I'm sure this boy told you a few juicy tales.

CENDRARS: I'll tell you, what amused me far more than dining with the stars or drinking with the starlets at the Tour Eiffel or the Concorde, or dancing at Louis Prime, the fashionable nightclubs of those times, was to loiter the day away in the sewing shops of the studios where I saw the mannequins of these women, the bust riddled with coloured needles and pins, covered with pen and pencil markings on the back and the index cards riddled with figures on the hips, marking their physiological decrepitude, or, on the contrary, the zenith of their bursting sumptuousness, or the full plumpness of their age, and all of it charted and recorded like accounting books. As an invasion of privacy, pretty hard to surpass. It was fascinating. I took no end of notes and measurements.

MANOLL: So, you have no recollection of the stories that Thomson told you?

CENDRARS: I didn't tell any in my articles in *Paris-Soir*. I merely drew a portrait of the masseur.

MANOLL: You sketched his portrait?

CENDRARS: He was a very handsome lad, in passing.

MANOLL: So, a very beautiful young boy, who undoubtedly had a lot of good fortune, and adventures.

CENDRARS: Of course, goes without saying. But he wouldn't breathe a word. He is discreet. *Motus!* is his byword.

MANOLL: One thing that you should share with us is your visit to the jeweller of the Hollywood stars. It's a highly unusual tale. You passed by there…

CENDRARS: But everything is curious and unusual from a marketing standpoint in the United States. For example: you enter a large department store, the way we might walk into *Galeries Lafayette* in

Paris, to purchase a gift for your mother-in-law, and you're not sure what to choose. There's a special counter called the *Suggestion* counter, staffed by an exquisite looking salesgirl. You explain your predicament. "What, sir, it's for mummy-in-law? You give this to mummy-in-law, you give that to mummy-in-law…" and you leave with a pile under your arms and absolutely thrilled with your purchases.

MANOLL: That reminds me of the Chicago cemetery, with electrical organs, gramophones to sing psalms and the deceased exposed in the parlour, dressed fashionably, the nails clipped and with the latest make-up. Have you ever come across that?

CENDRARS: No, I've never seen that. You can't see everything. But the Hollywood cemetery isn't too bad either. It's located on a parcel of land on the periphery of Los Angeles and Hollywood, a lot planted with admirable cypresses. Every night, a neon sign lights up and flashes out a message: "What are you waiting for? We're all doing fine here? Come quick! There are still a few places left…"

MANOLL: Have you seen these fetish objects being distributed in Hollywood?

CENDRARS: They're very costly. It's an underground market.

MANOLL: They sell Greta Garbo's teeth?

CENDRARS: Greta Garbo's baby teeth and Mae West's canines. It's such a scurvy trade that a lad such as Robert Florey, a Frenchman who has been in Hollywood for more than thirty years, keeps a log book, a secret chronicle of Hollywood, a curious journal, up on all the gossip and the latest scandal of the studios. He once thanked me for having told him about this tale, with a few addresses of boutiques which he could sink his teeth into. Since that time, he's built up his own collection of Hollywood fetishes. The prize piece in his collection is inside a box, the small moustache that Chaplin used to keep attached by an elastic band.

MANOLL: Yet another indiscreet question.

CENDRARS: Manoll, let's not talk about Hollywood anymore. The pre-war cinema is dead and its international celebrities are already old fogies. Amen.

MANOLL: A final question…

CENDRARS: Shoot.

MANOLL: I wanted to ask you, Cendrars, why you no longer do any cinema and why you don't do more of it.

CENDRARS: I fell out of love with it Manoll. Me and the cinema, we got a divorce on grounds of incompatibility.

IX

Boozing with Hemingway

MANOLL: When you travelled to Hollywood on assignment, my dear Blaise Cendrars, didn't you stop by in Chicago?

CENDRARS: No. I didn't stop by, it was too cold, end of February and one of those blizzards coming through! Besides, it was a city that I already knew, and like all the big American cities, Chicago can bore you to death. San Francisco is the same thing, and it's probably the most sympathetic capital of the United States. So, in the end, it's unsustainable, you just can't live in the United States. Just think, that when I came in 1936 to Hollywood to carry out my assignment, it was twenty-five years after my first arrival in the City of Angels. It's another city now. And at that time, neither Hollywood or the cinema existed. Otherwise, I probably would have stayed. Hollywood was a suburb, the "Wood of Hollies" suburb, thus its name. As for Los Angeles, it's the most mortal city in America. They commit serial suicides. And yet, I adore the United States. I go there as often as possible. I have always advised friends to spend one month per year in America instead of spending their month in Switzerland enjoying the fresh air. Because in America, you can ventilate the mind. You have no idea how life in America can take strange turns. In my case, I love New York. I go there as often as possible to undergo a laugh cure. That city has me cracking up from morning until night, and from night until morning. I can't bring myself to take these Americans seriously.

MANOLL: It's the architecture.

CENDRARS: It's everything. It's the American way of life. It's not the structure of American life per se, which isn't too bad as a social fantastic and which beats by far anything a Pierre MacOrlan or a Wells could dream up as a horrific vision of the future, no. But it's life, day-to-day life, the appearance of people in the street, the conception of people who all follow the same cues. You can see it in their facial expressions. People who all think the same thing. People who all read the same newspapers and who all look so contented. In the subway, they're all dressed in the same way, as if they came off the production line. Based on their clothing, just their outer appearance, you can know where they live. You can calculate their subway stop. You can already figure out their trade, how much they earn, whether they are living too high on the hog, their neighbourhood or borough. It's amusing no end.

MANOLL: New York is the city you know best?

CENDRARS: To give you an idea, I went there nine times in a row in 1938, for the week-end, for four days and four nights, between the outgoing and incoming trip of the *Normandie*.

MANOLL: You didn't take the plane.

CENDRARS: I was in no hurry. I took the week-end off – a twelve-day weekend actually, voyage included. I didn't go to carry on business. I went there to have a laugh. I was fed up with Paris and politics.

MANOLL: And the other cities?

CENDRARS: I know them. But I adore New York. I spend my time cracking up in New York. It's a very funny place, provided you don't have to hold down a job or make money, nor accumulate any money. Then it's hell…

MANOLL: Was it in New York that you met Hemingway?

CENDRARS: No. In the *Closerie des Lilas*[115] in Paris.

MANOLL: Under what circumstances?

CENDRARS: Under no particular circumstances. I was having a drink. He was having a drink at the next table. He was with an American sailor on leave. He was in some kind of uniform; I forget which one, probably in the uniform of a volunteer orderly, unless I'm mistaken. I had already been amputated. It was near the end of the other war, the war to end all wars. There was some back and forth between the tables. Drunks love to blab. You blab. You drink. You clink glasses. You re-clink and you drink. I had to leave for a meeting up in Montmartre, with the widow of a friend, André Dupont, a poet killed at Verdun. I used to drop by his place every Friday to eat *bouillabaisse* with Satie, Georges Auric, Paul Lombard, and sometimes, Max Jacob. I would bring my boozy American friends to give them a nice plate properly cooked up. But Americans don't like properly cooked food. They don't have any cuisine in America. They don't even know what it is. Hemingway and his sailor weren't open to my arguments. They preferred to slake their thirst. So, I dumped them in a bar on *rue des Martyrs*, I forget which one, and I left for a feast at the home of my friend's widow. Satie was already there, Auric as well. Paul Lombard wore an apron and he shouted for joy every time he tasted the *coulis au safran*. After dinner, we stayed well into the night to redact the fashion chronicle that our well-heeled friend, the lovely Valentine, wrote in a daily and that she signed *Les Caquets de Dame Peluche*. It would be interesting to dig up those sheets.

MANOLL: Did Hemingway translate anything of yours?

CENDRARS: No, but John Dos Passos[116] translated *Le Panama* in 1931.

MANOLL: John Dos Passos also devoted a chapter to you in *Orient-Express* and called you the *Homer of the Transsiberian*. He's a friend of yours?

CENDRARS: When John got married, I was in the Périgord. I was in the process of cobbling together my book on Galmot.[117] He came through on his honeymoon, from New York directly to Monpazier, Galmot's birthplace. It was a fortified *bastide* home constructed by some kings of England, dating from 1426. It is very small, six hundred and twenty-five residents maximum. It has the layout of an American city. There are two principal arterial roads at right angles. You could number the addresses just like in America. I think there are twenty-one. I was lodged in the best hotel of the region, the *Hôtel de Londres,* where the eating was celestial, an eatery held by Madame Cassagnol. Her husband is the spitting image of Chaplin. Madame Casagnol wore the moustache and trousers in the household. When John Dos Passos announced his arrival to me, I said to Madame Cassagnol: "I have some friends coming directly from New York to your establishment. See if you can't outdo yourself." And I didn't give it another thought, either to the menu or to the wine cellar. For eight days, Madama Cassagnol prepared this fine *Périgourdine* cuisine for us, wrote up the menus, everything in ascending order, surprising us every day with truffles, *pot-au-feu à l'ail pour faire chabrot,** *buisson d'écrevisses* [garnished crayfish], mushroom in cream sauce, *cèpes à la bordelaise*, fried fish from the Dordogne and from the Garonne, skewers of small birds, snipefish *à l'armagnac*, small fur and winged game, venison caught by poachers, the principal supplier being the curé of the village, roasts, *terrine de foie gras*, wild lettuce salads, peasant cheeses, figs stuffed with honey and ground nuts, Agen prunes, *crêpes flambées*, bottomless flagons of red plonk, a bottle of Monbazillac for two, coffee, liqueurs, all for a total cost of twelve francs fifty, fifty-five centimes extra for the surprise of the eighth day. I didn't even know that there were still whooper swans in France, even migratory swans. The Black Périgord is truly a stunning area.

MANOLL: What do you think of wild swan? How was it prepared?

---

* convivial practice in the Southwest where you pour some wine into the remaining juice of the stew, and then drink it straight from the plate.

CENDRARS: It was succulent, stuffed to the gills and presented in the royal manner, with all the tail feathers stuffed up its behind, forming a cartwheel.

MANOLL: Did you not see Dos Passos again?

CENDRARS: I saw John frequently, but only in Paris. It's curious, but I never, never, never saw any of my American writer friends in the United States despite my numerous sojourns in the country. They were AWOL. Coincidentally, when I insisted on the telephone, the person responding would invariably inform me that the master I was trying to track down was either on vacation, doing a tour, or even in Europe. I attempted in vain to track one or the other down at newspaper offices, at the club, or at his publishing house. The response was everywhere the same: "Nobody's home!" I would always hang up with a bizarre feeling. I don't want to draw any adverse conclusions about anybody, but I ended up admitting deep down inside that American writers are not free in their own land, and that those returning from Europe don't have a clear conscience, feeling guilt for their mischievous forays, the recollection of which would be painful for them. They are afraid of public opinion and don't have the stomach to return a courtesy, contrary to the English. It's a typically American complex.

MANOLL: So, among the American writers, you knew Henry Miller. Was he a close friend of yours?

CENDRARS: Henry Miller? I met him in Paris. I never saw him anywhere but in Paris.[118] A droll fellow. A pal and a crony. Un *joyeux compagnon*. A merry prankster.

MANOLL: Did you run into any of the others?

CENDRARS: They were impossible to miss, these poets. They'd drift in and hang around and then disappear and you'd never hear from them again. I've forgotten their names. Paris was overrun with them just before the last war broke out.

MANOLL: They say you were a reference for them, that you had a massive influence on certain American authors.

CENDRARS: Me? What a load of rubbish. Categorically false. If I had any influence on any of them, I wasn't aware of it and none of them was aware of it, so I don't see how that adds up to me being a reference. You want to know something? Victor Hugo and Maupassant, now those two were references for the writers who set up shop in Paris at the end of the other war. They all came to France on impulse, either as soldiers or ambulance drivers or diplomats. When the war ended, they stayed for varying lengths of time; some of them set up camp for the entire inter-war period. They hung out at Montparnasse, then at Saint-Germain-des-Près. I'll tell you if they were influenced by anything it was by the atmosphere. You could breathe in Paris then. They were influenced by the French way of life far more than by any French writer. One day, John Dos Passos said to me: "In France you have a literary genre which doesn't exist in the United States. It's the *"grand reportage"* à la Victor Hugo. The coverage of major international events.

MANOLL: That's an incredible statement.

CENDRARS: I admit, I was stunned when I heard it. I'd always presumed that *reportage* was invented by the Americans. Apparently not! So, as far as reporting the big events goes, it appears that we are the ones who have exercised an influence on these young American novelists, who hadn't yet started writing for major newspapers and until then tended to quarter in their ivory towers, writing letters and attempting to write literature. They've certainly made up for lost time. Just look at the recent war reporting and other journalism of Seabrook,[119] Hemingway, or for that matter even John Dos Pass himself. Every one of them shows traces of this French influence and they are all superb writers. They reinvented the genre. Seabrook's *Asylum* is a masterpiece of this style of realistic reporting, much in the vein of Victor Hugo's *The Death of Balzac*, which was the first of the genre. Turns out Dos Passos was right.

MANOLL: What about Faulkner, did you ever meet him?

CENDRARS: No, I didn't know Faulkner. Never met the man. He never came to Paris. Malraux once asked me to write the preface for a translated version of *Light in August*. I declined. It was too provincial, too literary for me, written in a style that no longer exists. You could say he wrote *too* well. When I travelled to the United States, I didn't go to meet writers or novelists. I preferred to spend my time in the streets, mooching around with a lad who worked as a window-washer of skyscrapers. I used to scale these high-rises with him, right up to the highest floor. At night, he'd take me to Harlem, or some neighbourhood music-hall, or we'd hang out in a popular greasy spoon. Let me tell you something. There's so much misery in New York and there's such a collection of oddballs, but nobody talks about them anymore since O. Henry. I loved riding around day and night with this taxi driver. He'd drive through the sleazy quarters of the East Side while he told me stories, non-stop. The last time I went to New York, in 38, I didn't even take a room. I walked into the lobby at the Waldorf Astoria, sat down in an armchair, and I spent four days and four nights in the hall watching the City of New York parade by, drinking and chatting with all these society types, who filled me in on all the gossip of the city and gave me all the dirt on the scandals of the day. That's when I missed my chance for a once-in-a-lifetime piece.

MANOLL: Really! Tell me about it

CENDRARS: I'm not putting you on, just like Sinclair Lewis' story, this is another true tale. I found myself in the Waldorf Astoria around three or four am. The lobby was deserted. I slid into my usual armchair when this women spouts out of nowhere, takes a step, and a lighter appears, igniting a cigarette. The woman moves down towards the end of the lobby, and starts window-shopping for no particular reason in front of a showcase window for in front of some shops which were already closed, but whose showcase displays were garishly displayed. I couldn't help but notice and follow this woman. She was exquisitely dressed; you might even say a sober and refined elegance. But I don't know what it was in her that shocked me – the nape, her muscles, which the elegance of her dress couldn't camouflage, that the twist of her pearls didn't mitigate. Something authoritarian, athletic, male, which bothered me in her gait. Her steps, the gestures, and what penetrated right through to her simpering airs when she was arranging herself in front of a mirror, powdered herself, gazed into the mirror, re-applied her lipstick. I observed her with intensity, slid up behind her by a show window, spying on her discreetly and wondering, "Who is this?" and then recalling "Come on, Blaise me boy, watch your step! You're in the Waldorf Astoria. She could be a billionaire. She's got beautiful jewels. She's beautifully built. She is beautiful. She must be thirty-five years old. But what the hell is she doing here in the Waldorf at this time of night? Women aren't allowed in here. In Paris, a woman of this calibre, sculpted like a gymnast and supremely elegant, in the latest fashion style, could only be, can only be, is nothing but a circus rider who has married an old noble from an illustrious line, a duke, a prince, a Mortemart…But here, a king of New York, banker, financier, magnate of radio, cinema, automobile, tires, telephones, the king of something. And as if to confirm my speculations, the mysterious woman entered a corridor leading to the lift serving the tower of the billionaires. I was going to follow her when, as I'm rounding the corner into the corridor, Freddy, the barman[120] grabbed me by the arm, dragged me into his lair and said, "Don't rub up against that one, Mr Cendrars, it's the hotel detective!!…" And he poured me out a good whisky to console me over my disappointment. Thus, everything could be explained: her supreme elegance, since, by her profession, this woman had to be dressed to the nines in the manner of the wives of the billionaires whom she was stalking and with whom she mixed during their stay without sticking out like a sore thumb, her discreetly male demeanour, and highly trained gymnastic musculature, since this woman was a police officer, and as a good European, of course, the thought had never occurred to me. "Not to worry," I said to Freddy, "you shouldn't have warned me. I've now missed the best story of my entire career…"

MANOLL: But why, Cendrars?"

CENDRARS: What, haven't you understood, Manoll? Tell me, when would she have slapped the cuffs on me, before, during or after?

MANOLL: Ah! That's funny! But maybe she had a "crush" on you, Blaise…

CENDRARS: It's possible. I considered the possibility. I was really askew with the notion of this adventure, yet that could have caused such a scandal and given me such a huge push forward in my nascent career as a reporter and make me an overnight celebrity in America because of the earth-shaking consequences...Believe me, Manoll, an adventure of this type is a lot more interesting for the novelist that I am than dining inside a club of intellectuals or academics, or even the XXth Century-Club which is a very closed circle, an exclusive club of American francophiles, as a matter of fact so francophile that it looks like a shooting gallery. All these old fogey founders and members of this club where I was invited to lunch, on the day prior to my departure by my American publisher, who, after three years of reflections, returned the favour of a lunch that I had offered him chez Dagorno in Paris and where we had drunk far too much, to such a point in fact that after the lunch, at the Bourget, my publisher boarded the plane for Amsterdam instead of the plane for London, where he was travelling urgently, if memory serves me correctly to negotiate the memoirs of H.G. Wells, the old fogeys putting on their French airs, with moustaches, goatees, sideburns, heads so completely outmoded that they must have been inspired by obsolete outdated reviews of Second Empire hair stylists, dandy Frenchies like you still see in certain Hollywood films. They really are going overboard a bit, but they looked happy and oh, so proud! The comical thing is that they were all engineers, architects, businessmen and even distinguished attorneys! As a phenomenon of inflated sentimentality, pretty hard to beat. I won't dwell on it, but they don't admit women to the club.

MANOLL: Isn't there a neighbourhood in New York which resembles *St-Germain-de Près*, where aesthetes and poets meet?

CENDRARS: No.

MANOLL: I think it's in the suburbs. A village where only artists live?

CENDRARS: You must be referring to Greenwich Village. It's in New York, lower Manhattan. It's an artists' quarter, filled with the literary club crowd, especially single women, but nothing to do with *Saint-Germain-de-Près*!

MANOLL: Weren't you curious to check it out?

CENDRARS: No. I don't frequent those people. The less you know of them the better; they're painful bores, aesthetes. A friend, a Hungarian Jew, a publicity agent, invited me one night to dine out to introduce me to his young fiancée. The taxi driver didn't even know where it was, it's such a forgotten, moss-stinking neck of the city, the artists' quarter of New York. The concierge of this young couple, an old French peasant who had already been in New York for more than forty years, learning that her young employers were going to receive a Frenchman to dine, put on an atrocious scene because there was no wine ready for the occasion of my visit. She dipped into her own savings to go out and purchase god knows how many dozens of kilos of grapes to make the typical wine of her region. I was very moved by this gesture.

MANOLL: So, you did drink some French wine while there.

CENDRARS: Which was very poor quality, rancid actually, but that was of little account. It was the intent of the old servant that counted. A New York janitor making Burgundy in the manner of her native village!

MANOLL: And, where did you live in Paris prior to the war?

CENDRARS: *Avenue Montaigne.* It's an amazing quarter that I know well. I lived at number 12, 60, 51, 33, 5 and finally I came back to the 12. I could write a book on this quarter which in appearance is so tranquil, with its proper, law-abiding citizens, and yet where things happen, things you wouldn't believe! I even found a title for this book: *Voyage autour de l'Alma* (Voyage around the Alma). But I'll probably never write it,[121] just like I won't write a lot of other books I've been daydreaming about for years.

MANOLL: What is your favourite memory of the Alma?

CENDRARS: I couldn't say; there's so many. That's the place where my good friends, the sewer-men of the City of Paris carry out their breeding of dog ratters in a subterranean ratodrome. There was also a Don Juan sweeper who seduced all the skivvies of the avenue and locked himself inside the Morris columns with them where he had installed a red velvet cushion. Just opposite is the Brazilian embassy where I used to finish off my nights drinking *cafezinhos*, smoking cigars and Dantas, nicknamed the Bohemian ambassador because he didn't have any bed. When fatigue got the better of him, he pushed up the collar of his jacket, stuck a hat on his skull and stretched out on a canapé made of Russian leather, closed his eyes and fell asleep like a child, without even seeing you out the door. In 1913, I even wrote a small book on Russian music[122] for the inauguration of the *Grand-Théâtre des Champs-Elysées*. During the gala evening of the *Rite of Spring* (23 May 1913),[123] a woman nearby, covered by diamonds, but the music of Stravinsky drove her crazy, tore out a brand new folding seat and smashed me over the head with it, so I had to spend the rest of the night drinking champagne in Montmartre with Stravinsky, Diaghilev, male and female dancers of the Russian Ballet troupe, still wearing the folding chair like a horse collar, my face a grate of bloody scratches. I saw the quarter evolve, the fashion designers – from Madeleine Vionnet to Boyd – set up shop there. *Francis*, which was then called *A la vue de la Tour Eiffel* was a bistrot for hackney coachmen. It had been transformed into a "Grill Room". Taxis had replaced hackney cabs; Bugatti, Jouvet opened *La Comédie Française*, Batbedat *le Studio*, Héberto operated the Perret theatre, construction to be ready to produce Parsifal as soon as the opera of Richard Wagner fell into the public domain. Freelancing at Bayreuth using a steam printer stored in the basement, which had cost millions but had never been used, a deluxe music-hall where all of Paris flocked, not to mention the Swedish ballets of Rolf de Maré, who produced a *bal nègre* – *La Création du Monde*, with music of Darius Milhaud and the settings and props done by Fernand Léger, Cocteau's *Wedding at the Eiffel Tower*, Erik Satie's *Relâche*. I actually wrote the publicity for old Satie and then Francis Picabia swiped the idea, the subject and the cinematographic creation of *Entr'acte* (Intermission) which allowed René Clair to make his debuts as a director, since Picabia took advantage of me being away in Brazil.[124] You see, it was quite an era…

MANOLL: Among all these unusual characters for whom you clearly have such affection, who did you meet in Paris?

CENDRARS: The most curious I met on avenue Montaigne was this crazy woman who inspired Giraudoux for his *Madwoman of Chaillot*; It wasn't the *"Môme aux Bijoux"* of Montmartre as claimed in the newspapers of the time, accompanied by the photo of this old, broken hussy with the troubled past that Jean Giraudoux used to create the central character of *The Madwoman of Chaillot.* Leffray was in fact an English woman. She was the widow of a well-heeled Cockney coachman. She lived on *rue Lauriston.* I used to follow her around. She would walk every day from the Chaillot down to avenue Montaigne, where she would take a seat on a bench just opposite the Plaza Athénée and she remained there in a state of ecstasy, dolled up like the Moreno[125] and she was so good at replicating his model, with that precise expression, slightly taller than Moreno, but much thinner, soiled ostrich feathers perched on her felt hat, with flea-market trinkets and baubles, a long gigot-sleeved dress full of holes and lace, the remains of a tatty, ermine stole that looked like a rack of shredded, indigo tails, extravagant stiletto heels, gloves running without end up her arms, grotesque jewellery, opera glasses, a handbag which hung down to the ground. The whole quarter knew her and teased her. She was truly mad as a hatter. Never addressed so much as a word to anyone, and refused to be interviewed. She had her aloofness, and was disdainful, full of haughtiness. It was there, enthroned on her bench which is no longer there today, that Giraudoux must have seen her as frequently as I since Jean was in the neighbourhood on a daily basis.

MANOLL: Because of the *Comédie des Champs-Elysées*?

CENDRARS: Exactly, which was a hop and a skip from the bench of the madwoman. That's where Giraudoux and Jouvet made their real debuts as men of the theatre.

MANOLL: Tell me, Cendrars, I would like to know, when did you first move to Paris. Right after your return from the war of 14, or did you continue vagabonding after?

CENDRARS: Of course, I travelled. I haven't stopped vagabonding to the present day.

MANOLL: You only stayed for brief sojourns in Paris?

CENDRARS: Yes and no. I stayed and I didn't stay.

MANOLL: You mean to say you lived a little bit all over the place.

CENDRARS: At one time or another, I lived in all the arrondissements of Paris. After spending a month in an arrondissement, I would move onto the next. But I always kept a fixed address, *avenue Montaigne, rue de Savoie, rue du Mont-Dore, rue Pétrarque*, where I still dropped by to pick up my mail. I'd do my rounds.

MANOLL: You also lived in several suburbs of Paris. You once said twenty-six different localities.

CENDRARS: I've never really added them all up.

MANOLL: It's mentioned towards the end of "Panama" or "Transsibérien". Not that it matters.

CENDRARS: At that time, I often travelled to the suburbs and beyond. I didn't have a bicycle or a motor vehicle. I took the train. I'd jump on at the first train station I came across. I'd stay for an hour or so on a direct, which would get me to Rambouillet, Melun and so forth. Then I'd climb onto a tourist train and I'd allow myself to be led around for a half hour or so, then disembark, finally walk out of the train station, stroll for a quarter of an hour on a trunk road, zig to the left, zag to the right, cut onto a sideroad crossing, take a trail, and at the end of five minutes, I could bet that I'd discover a historical site, and emerge onto one of these magnificent and grandiose, but rarely visited sites, or even unknown or forgotten locations which are everywhere outside the Paris ring road, in Ile-de France just like in the Beauvais, the Multien, the Brie, the Gâtinais. That's how I discovered Saint-Martin-en-Bière, where I bought my first house in 1912. During those times, this entire bordering region at the extreme periphery of the Parisian metropolis was being sold for one sou per metre, built-up or vacant, with marvellous cottages, and better than cottages, castles. I organized a buyback for the Countess of T..., who was a close friend, the castle of her ancestors, something like seventy hectares, for one sou per meter, castle included, in a perfect state of conservation and in part furnished. The library still contained a large part of her books.

These *arriviste* landowners, who no longer cultivated their lands, abandoned the region, preferring to live in Paris, to wear the fake removable collar and the cravate and to take the metro, which had just been built, or on the tramways which were on the verge of disappearing. The farms, the windmills, the ironworks fell into states of ruin, fields left uncultivated, the assets forsaken, and this entire peasant civilisation dating from antiquity returned to nature. The orchards, the vines, the crops abandoned, the boundary markers erased by thorns. In the deserted villages, there remained only elderly men and women, and the grandchildren, the goitrous, the barmy and the idiots. For a collector of the human species, there was more than enough to hold your interest. You could take these day-trips repeatedly. Unforgettable days. And, a bag full of tales to tell upon my return.

MANOLL: And so you'd just wander about the whole day.

CENDRARS: There was a time when I possessed somewhere around twenty-seven houses in the countryside, all over the place, and not only in the region surrounding Paris, but much further. I would purchase a peasant shack for about a thousand *balles,** set up a camping cot, hang up a lamp, haul in a few boxes of books…

MANOLL: Do you recall…

CENDRARS: …I'd unpack my cookware in aluminium. Simple as that. You could leave the key in the door behind you, and no worries about thieves. No doubt about it.

MANOLL: Do you remember all these houses that you had in every corner of the land?

CENDRARS: Of course I remember.

MANOLL: You'd visit them randomly?

CENDRARS: Depending on my desires, on a whim, how I felt on any particular day, the weather, the season. Eventually, I purchased a Fiat automobile. I used to drive a lot.

---

* former slang term for francs

CENDRARS SPEAKS

MANOLL: When war was declared in 14, didn't you co-sign with Canudo[126] a call to foreigners, friends of France, bidding them to enlist? This appeal, published in all the newspapers of Paris, apparently yielded spectacular results.

CENDRARS: Yes. Eighty-thousand foreign volunteers enlisted in France during the war of '14.

MANOLL: That is when you enlisted in the Foreign Legion?

CENDRARS: You couldn't very well enlist anywhere else.

MANOLL: Yes. You said that, contrary to many people who wielded a pen, you didn't engage in war to write about it, because at that time, you were a soldier and you had a rifle in your hand...

CENDRARS: That's why I could never be part of – and still can never today be part of – any group of writer-soldiers. You are a soldier or you are a writer. When you write, you don't fight with a gun, and when you're firing a rifle, you're not writing. You write after. It would have been better to write before and to have prevented all that...

MANOLL: That's what you said about Apollinaire.

CENDRARS: Begging your pardon, but he also enlisted.

MANOLL: You read his war poems and you declared that you would have been incapable of writing in the midst of the action as he had done.

CENDRARS: Ah, so that's it? *Eh bien*! I can tell you that the war didn't inspire me in the least from a poetic standpoint. What amazes me is that someone like Apollinaire, to cite but one – there have been others since, for example, Aragon, on May 10, 1940, – was able to compose rhymes in the trenches, to write frilly little poems, sentimental little odes, pleasing little landscapes. Heart-warming little gentlemen.

MANOLL: If the war didn't inspire you to write poetry, it nevertheless spawned numerous tales.

CENDRARS: I wrote several accounts. I even wrote a book on the war, but thirty years later.

MANOLL: That is what is astonishing. You allowed so much time to pass prior to writing it.

CENDRARS: If I had written in the aftermath of the war, it would have been quite a different book, much more visual, photographic, instantaneous, but not truer to life for all that. The synthesis, the portrait requires that you step back. That you forget. Also that you forgive!…

MANOLL: In any event, in this book, you render a true homage to the Legion. You say this: "I owe to the Legion my apprenticeship of solitude and through the Legion; I learned what it was to be a man. I learned the craft of being a man…"

CENDRARS: A handyman.

MANOLL: *The Severed Hand* is a magnificent book.

CENDRARS: …rather than a man of the pen.

MANOLL: All these characters you evoke – the London sewer man, Colon, the Canadian, Garnéro…

CENDRARS: I buried them alive those men.

MANOLL: You forgot a few. In *The Shattered Man*, you added a few names to the list.

CENDRARS: It's possible. I cannot recall all these fine men who paraded by. There were so many in the squadron, more than two hundred of them. Today, three of us still survive.

MANOLL: There's something else in *The Severed Hand*, something I could call an Honours and Shame List. Let me remind you of the episode. A policeman comes to investigate you. He's somebody who knows all the Montparnos. You ask him for news of your friends. He responds: *Braque is at the front. Léger is at the front. Derain is at the front. Modigliani is still drinking like a fish in Montparnasse. Delaunay has gone off to Spain. Today, he's in Madrid. Picasso stopped at the Spanish border. Picabia has left for America…, etc.*" [127] *With no added commentary.*

CENDRARS: No additional commentary was necessary.

MANOLL: Come on! They could have fought!

CENDRARS: Easy to say. Picabia is Cuban. Picasso is Spanish. Delaunay didn't feel like coming. He had no desire to be a soldier. He was reformed at the French embassy in Madrid. There had to be a few who didn't participate in this war, to save our honour, as you phrase the case so well.

MANOLL: Ah! You are a nasty louse!

CENDRARS: "War causes turbulent people to disappear," I once heard from the mouth of a Chinese peasant, "but the whiners remain behind." As for me, I have nothing to say...you're the nasty and vicious one. Another who had nothing to say was Erik Satie.[128] During a night of bombing during 1918, one of the last and most violent of the war, I found a man prostate at the foot of the Obelisk, *Place de la Concorde*. I leaned over him, believing he was dead. It was old Satie. "And what are you doing there?" I asked him. He responded: "I know it's ridiculous and I'm not in a shelter. What do you think, this thing here rises into the sky, and I feel like I'm in a shelter. So, I am composing a music for the Obelisk. Don't you think that a fine thing?" "Yes," I responded. "As long as it isn't a military march." "*Ah, bon!*" he retorts, "no danger of that. It's music for the Pharaoh who is buried beneath. Nobody ever thinks about him. It took this bitch of a bombing attack to get me here. It's the first time. I'm telling you, it's not bad, this whole business..." And he laughed, hand in his beard, as usual, his malicious eyes measuring the monument..."Do you know who is buried beneath?" I asked Satie. Apparently, the mummy of Cleopatra. At least, that's what I have heard...– "Not possible," says Satie. So, I was right to compose my little ditty. Listen:

Ta, tarâ, ta, ta, ta, ta, ta
ta, tarâ, ta, ta, ta, ta...
Fa, do-ô, sol, ré, la, I, si –Fa, do-o, sol, ré, la, mi."

X

Apollinaire's Funeral

MANOLL: Blaise Cendrars, tell me more about Guillaume Apollinaire.

CENDRARS: What else do you need to know about poor Apollinaire?

MANOLL: Well, first of all, why do you always refer to him as "poor" Guillaume?

CENDRARS: Because he's on the wrong side of the fence.

MANOLL: What do you mean, 'the wrong side?'

CENDRARS: The Netherworld. The Realm of Shadows.

MANOLL: The Empire of the dead?

CENDRARS: No. You heard what I said. I said. *The Realm of Shadows*. That's why I dislike talking about Guillaume Apollinaire…[129]

MANOLL: Why? Weren't you at his burial?

CENDRARS: As a matter of fact, something so extraordinary happened to me at his burial, that even now after thirty-two years, I find it difficult to believe that he's dead.

MANOLL: What precisely are you saying, Cendrars?

CENDRARS: What? Don't tell me you believe he's dead?

MANOLL: Of course, *hélas*!

CENDRARS: So, obviously, Manoll, you've never read *L'enchanteur Pourrissant (The Rotting Wizard).*[130]

MANOLL: *The Rotting Wizard*?

CENDRARS: I recommend it. It's *the* key book to understanding Apollinaire. The book that contains all the secrets of poor Guillaume…

MANOLL: What secrets?

CENDRARS: The secrets of his genius. The secrets of his evocative genius. I'll tell you what. The secrets of his double, no, his triple nature!

MANOLL: But what happened to you at Apollinaire's burial that's making you all of a sudden start talking about him in this way?

CENDRARS: Let me tell you about the funeral. The priest had just given absolution. Just by the St Thomas Aquinas portico, the coffin of Apollinaire emerged, draped with the French flag. We pushed the coffin inside the hearse. Guillaume's lieutenant képi was placed on the tricoloured flag, clearly displayed among the crowns and the flowers. The guard of honour – a demi-squadron of *poilus* regulars, weapons held under the arm – lined up, and the convoy rumbled along slowly, the family moving slowly on foot behind the vehicle. His mother, his wife were wearing mourning veils. Poor Jacqueline had barely escaped the Spanish flu epidemic herself that had taken away Guillaume. She was barely away from her own death bed, and absolutely shattered. The intimate friends of Apollinaire were also there – Prince Jastrebzoff, Serge, his sister, the baroness of Oettingen,[131] Max Jacob, Picasso, all the other friends of Guillaume, including Pierre Albert-Birot[132] and his wife who did everything short of slitting open her veins to produce *Les Mamelles de Tirésias* in *Théâtre Maubel*, the whole of the Parisian world of letters, arts, the print media, but then, as the cortège turned onto boulevard Saint Germain, it was assaulted by booing and jeers coming from an out-of-control crowd cut loose of the most recent mob of protesters celebrating the Armistice, men and women arm-in-arm, singing, dancing, embracing each other and howling in delirium the famous refrain of the end of the war:

> *...Nay, ya shouldn'a done it, you shouldn'a done it, Guillaume,*
> *Nay, you shouldn'a gone, you shouldn'a gone to war.*

It was extremely painful. And, behind me, I could hear the old fogies, the last fossils of symbolism, all these immortal poets utterly forgotten today, clucking away and gossiping with each other about the future of Poetry and asking what the young poets would now become after the death of Apollinaire. They were fairly exulting, as if they had just won the battle between the Ancients and the Moderns. It was atrocious, disgusting and I could feel the bile rising and anger getting the better of me. So, before I yielded to my urge to stir up some trouble I pulled rank at the Boul' Mich intersection and abandoned the cortège; Raymone and Fernand Léger accompanied me. We ducked into the first bistro for a hot grog to at least warm ourselves up enough so we didn't come down with the flu ourselves. After downing a stand-up grog, we jumped into a taxi. When we arrived at Père-Lachaise, we found that the whole burial ceremony which had been proceeding on foot had somehow beaten us to destination. Don't ask me how, but somehow between the traffic jams and the Armistice bands dancing at every street corner, the procession had arrived, the ceremony had been held and Apollinaire's friends were already dispersing. I asked Paul Fort where the tomb was. Based on his extremely vague directions, we started our own hike through the tombs and the cenotaphs, Raymone, Fernand and myself, until we finally fell across two freshly dug graves. The two gravediggers were taking a break from their work. We asked them where we could find Apollinaire's grave. They had no idea – "You have to understand, sir, between the Spanish flu and the war, nobody tells us the names of the bodies we're bringing down into the hole. There's just too many corpses for that. Maybe somebody up at the administration can help you. We don't have time, sorry. We're too wiped out." "But listen," I said, "it's a lieutenant, Lieutenant Guillaume Apollinaire or Kostrowitsky. They must have fired a gun salute at graveside!" "Listen old man," said the foreman. "Two volleys were fired, sir! Both graves were for lieutenants, see? How are we supposed to know who's who? Why don't you check it out for yourself?" We leaned over and gazed into the graves. They were already half filled-in. Nothing distinguished them. The bouquets and sprays of flowers had already disappeared, already swiped by street hawkers who refashioned them into bouquets. These hawkers worked Paris cemeteries city-wide, stole the flowers, then resold them in the metro during the evenings. We were just ready to withdraw when I noticed a clump of turf with a few sprouts of grass in the bottom of one of the two tombs. "Look," I said to Raymone and to Fernand Léger, "look, it's prodigious!! You'd swear it was Apollinaire's head…" The rolled up frozen cylinder of turf in the bottom of the hole had exactly the same form as Apollinaire's head and the grass was planted in exactly the same pattern as his hair during his lifetime, routing its way around the scar where they had perforated his skull. And this was no illusion brought on by hypnosis. As is usually the case when an inanimate thing starts to agitate, indicating it wants to re-enter the realm of the living, the psychic energies can get pretty intense. You don't have to hallucinate to not believe what you're actually seeing. We beat a retreat in haste. Raymone was weeping. Fernand was biting his lips. I waited until we were already out of the cemetery. There was a glacial fog enshrouding the monuments, pillars and cairns. I said: "It was him, no doubt. We all saw him. Apollinaire isn't dead. Pretty soon, he's going to make an appearance. Mark my words..." And, during the return trip, I recited to Raymone and Fernand remnants and fragments from *The Rotting Wizard* which seemed to be triggered in my mind by the rhythms of the jolts and bumps and the gear-shifting of the bus, hurtling down from Ménilmontant like Courtille driving the horse carriage of Milord l'Arsouille on a feast day. It was fantastical. Paris was madly celebrating. Apollinaire was a goner. I was consumed by melancholy. It was absurd. I often returned to inspect the platform of our vehicle. What mask would Guillaume be wearing to join in the festivities of his beloved Paris? Fernand Léger had a rendez-vous. Raymone was acting that evening in the *Théâtre de Belleville*. I wandered until midnight along *rue de Belleville, rue de Crimée, Place des Fêtes*, rubbing shoulders with the crowds so I could see them close-up. Then I took up a position at the artists' exit in the end of the cul-de-sac. When Raymone arrived, we returned home furtively. Where did I live? In the *Hôtel Mirabeau, rue de la Paix*. I still had eight days left in Paris. Now, it was me instead of Apolli-naire correcting the proofs and giving the OK to print the *Flâneur des Deux Rives*, which I had been editing for La Sirène. I returned to Nice where I was awaited to finish a film I was making. The wheel never stops turning. Poor Guillaume! The following year, in 1919, I published another book by him at La Sirène – the small edition of the *Bestiaire ou cortège d'Orphée*, with the woodcut prints of Dufy, but do you know what leaves me disconsolate? The fact that I never succeeded in editing the final book of Guillaume Apolli-naire that we had discussed at such great length together. The one that he finally wrote but for which he found no title. This book brought together within a single volume all his prefaces, notes, bi-ographies that he had written or hastily published, or even sum-marized in a collection of the *Maîtres de l'Amour* of the *Bibliothèque des Curieux, rue Furstenberg*,[133] entirely reviewed, revised and up-dated, sequenced, structured, edited and developed into a contin-uous whole, flowing like the current of an impetuous river. It was a prodigious book, which went far beyond the frontiers of simple cu-riosity or erudition. It wasn't an erotic book. It was the book of a poet. This work dazzled me. I found a title for it: *Styx*, after the name of the river of the Hades which circles the underworld seven times. Come to think of it, that's what it was. A black river, filled with tar and sulfur. The book still hasn't been published, but I find it hard to believe that the manuscript has been lost. What I mean by lost is lost for the world today. Maybe it has just been misplaced somewhere around *rue de Condé* or the library on *rue Furstenberg*. Actually, there's a better chance that it has fallen in the hands of bad councillors, that's what I really fear. So, there's still hope. I'm looking into it…

MANOLL: Thank you, Blaise Cendrars, for having related this story.

CENDRARS: It's the first time I've ever told it…

MANOLL: You've got to be joking.

CENDRARS: I'm telling you, first time ever.

MANOLL: And why is that?

CENDRARS: Because you have to be careful when you're dealing with necromancy. You have to watch what you say. In 1922, I had published an *Anthologies des grands occultistes (Anthology of the Great Wizards)* and Grillot de Givry[134] managed to get his hands on it using god knows what trickery and then by a further subterfuge succeeded in having his own name inserted instead of the author's. I happened to be in Rome at the time. Grillot de Givry was a celebrated occultist. He bragged that he was a magus, even a wizard. Several years later, he published *Le Musée des Sorciers, Mages et Alchimistes** with another publisher, abundantly illustrated. He even included an authentic portrait of Lucifer. There's a tale surrounding that portrait as well. Occultists are too afraid to reproduce it, upon pain of death. The magus received a message during the night, a warning. He decoded the signature during his sleep (I heard this detail straight from his mouth). The next day, he spent the entire morning chanting certain incantations and magical spells to free himself of the conspiracy that he felt was being hatched around him. After having taken a whole series of propitiatory and beneficial precautions, he stepped out, the work under his arm, and personally made the legal deposit of his book at the *Bib-*

---

* The Museum of Sorcerers, Magi and Alchemists

liothèque nationale. It was a dangerous endeavour and he knew it. He wore the seal of Salomon on the heart and a hair-shirt of thorns of Judas over his girth. As soon as his work was duly registered with the legal deposit official, he fled out the door like a criminal fugitive. But, Grillot de Givry was only able to make it across a courtyard, reeling as if drunk, stumbling, and then falling, struck down at the entrance of the *Bibliothèque nationale* without having made it as far as the street, where he only momentarily escaped the retaliation awaiting him. This exemplary death was much talked about in certain circles of occultists, magi and wizards who used to meet in *St-Germain de Près.*

MANOLL: Surely you're not suggesting that this sudden death is some kind of occult vengeance from the underworld…

CENDRARS: I wouldn't dream of it. The only person who could have intervened in this type of magical transaction is the Devil himself! Grillot de Givry was bound by a pact.

MANOLL: Come on!

CENDRARS: I stand by it. Don't tell me you don't believe in the old gentleman, Manoll?

MANOLL: …

CENDRARS: Just like Gogol, Apollinaire believed in him. It even haunted him. That's why he was so terrified of his neighbour, Doctor Mardrus,[135] the translator of *A Thousand and One Nights,* who lived on the floor beneath, boulevard St-Germain. Apollinaire accused him of sending him a black tomcat through the living room chimney, and of causing the weather vanes on his chimney to grind, which rose to the level of his terrace on the rooves, to put a spell on him, to trouble his spirit and bring him bad luck. He avoided him as much as possible, and when he met him, he'd break into shivers. As for the other joker, he'd be laughing silently. But, funny, it was Doctor Mardrus who invented the title *Caligrammes* for an album of figurative poems that Apollinaire had announced in an insert of the most recent issue of **Soirées de Paris**, under the title: *Anch'io son' pittore*!;

MANOLL: How amusing!

CENDRARS: You find this amusing? Not me. Already, before the war, I had given him the title for *Alcools*, but Apollinaire preferred *Eaux de Vies*, which he found more symbolic. He actually hung onto his own version right up until the final proofs of the *Mercure de France* edition. He finally changed it at the "OK to print" phase when he also decided to get rid of any punctuation.[136] But, after he returned from the front and after his trepanation, he was no longer the same man. He had become vain, childish, maudlin, impatient, proud, jealous, and outside of his sudden epiphany with *Styx*, he no longer produced anything grand and never again, outside of a few sparks of the old flame, did I see him spontaneous and joyful like in the old days. He was angst-ridden, full of apprehension for the future and came to believe in his misfortune. It was around that time that he became a censor at the instigation of André Billy. What a disaster for a creator like him! *Quos vult Jupiter Perdere, dementat prius*. I can well understand that he wanted to hang on to his rank of lieutenant, and his veteran's pay to cover his material needs. But, because he was soliciting the *Croix de guerre*,* he had a tendency to "officialise" his work and life and airbrush the scandals of other times like that absurd fiasco with the Mona Lisa, which got him fired from *Le Matin*, where he had published a weekly account on the theft of those Tanagras statuettes. And that cost him the Prix Goncourt right around the time of the publication of *L'Hérésiarque et Cie.*[137] After Cravan and the ridicule surrounding that botched up duel, people had started treating him as a Jew in the press. He wanted to rehabilitate himself in public opinion, make a career. That's why when he returned from the front, barely out of the clinic after his terrible injury, and notwithstanding his double trepanation, he took on the task of a daily column in Paris-Midi. It was the Foreign Press column, which meant he had to awaken every night in the pre-dawn so he could be at the newspaper offices by 4 am. Paris-Midi's early edition came out at 11 am. So, since he was already a night hawk, and never went to bed before midnight, he was being highly imprudent, particularly when you consider his terrible

---

* Military Cross

physical condition brought on by the numerous surgeries performed on him. Not to mention the permanent headaches he suffered from and that depleted all his resources. Then you tack on top of all that the burden and overwork down at the newspaper. One day he remarked to me "My poor Blaise, what do you expect me to do? I'm getting old. If I want to become famous, it's now or never. I want to become a celebrity. And for that, there's no other way. The public has to get used to seeing my name in the paper on a daily basis. That's why I took on this job. But it's tough…" Poor Guillaume! In 1918, I was shooting a film in Nice. In November, I'd come to Paris for eight days to find some fuel for my electrical generators that were out of service on the Riviera and to stock up on film that was in scarce supply. I also had to be in town to sign copies of a deluxe edition of *J'ai tué*, with illustrations by Léger, that François Bernouard[138] had to release that week. On Sunday, November 3, I coincidentally ran into Guillaume Apollinaire on *boulevard du Montparnasse* and we decided to have lunch together, between pals, at Père Baty, the best Bistro in the city at that time. We talked about the topic of the day, the Spanish flu epidemic that was taking out more victims than even the war. I had just crossed half of France in my vehicle and in the Lyon suburbs, I'd witnessed the incineration of plague victims who were being stacked in piles and then sprayed with petrol because the city was short of coffins. The picture was all the more desolate because in the freight area of the train station, factories were still burning in the wake of an air raid. I gave Apollinaire a tube of Harlem oil. I always kept supplies of it on me. I told him that I had already saved a lot of people with this drug that only cost twenty sous. Actually, it was nothing more than an extract of the famous catnip or common valerian, used in medical practices as an anti-pyretic remedy for spastics. It's frequently used in the Far East for female ailments and among Parisians of the lower classes for diseases of the spinal cord. In fact, it is the sole remedy of the Middle Ages which is still listed officially in the Codex. The formula for it is credited to Paracelsus. I pointed out to him that the prospectus, printed in red and black, opened with a prayer in Gothic characters addressed to Our Lord, which enveloped the small tube which bore the "Frothing horse"[139] seal, the mark of the current manufacturer in Harlem. The neck was sealed by a ring of parchment. I told him that he had put together all the components for a magnificent column and recommended he do a piece on Harlem oil, the sole effective remedy against the Spanish flu. A sensational piece in the next number of the *Mercure de France*. His column was called "The anecdotal life", a highly personal chronicle written by a jack-of-all-trades, very well informed, amusing and often biting satire. I'd even taken my short volume of the *Flâneur des Deux Rives** from it for my collections of **Tracts** published at **la Sirène**, which was being released at the end of the month…and by that time, Guillaume would already be dead and buried (alas, poor us!. And we took leave of each other on this Sunday the third in high spirits and very happy with each other. The week passed very quickly. Oyez: my fuel orders and film orders were liquidated in a few days. Things went more slowly chez Bernouard, who dawdled as usual and who couldn't keep his word. I was spending entire nights at Belle Edition giving a hand to Creisams,[140] the painter, an excellent colleague and crony who at that time was a typographer at Vernouard. We'd often work until dawn; the machine was running full steam ahead. Creixams monitored the printing press, the inking, slid the sheets under the roller. Using the composition stick, I corrected the misprints that this idiot, François-le-Berlue composed on purpose to authenticate his print runs (that's why he composed the title "I have killed" as "*J'ai tuè*" with the accent inverted, and I let him keep three copies with the inverted accent, which today must be worth their weight in gold!). Modigliani, who was with me most of the time, sketched our portraits or fell off into a drunken sleep amidst the bundles of paper. And here, Manoll, is the tragic calendar. I don't believe I'm in error on the dates in the mêlée of events which marked my sojourn in Paris. It was a couple of weeks that were so gruesomely pathetic, it would be impossible to erase them from memory. On Friday the 8th, after having broken bread with Creixams on *rue des Saints-Pères*, I dropped by to leave the first copy of *J'ai tué* which was hot off the press, with the concierge of Apollinaire. From the end of the corridor in her lodge, she shouted at me: "I've got the

---

* collections of chronicles

flu, don't come any further, I've got the flu! – "And, Apollinaire, is he there?" I asked. "I haven't seen Monsieur Apollinaire since Sunday." "And, madame?" "I haven't seen Madame Apollinaire for four or five days either." "Are you sure they're at home?" "Of course, I'm sure; they've got the flu, just like me. Don't go to see them!…" But, I was already running up the stairwell, taking the steps four at a time, and started ringing and ringing the doorbell, and beating on the door. After a very, very long time, Jacqueline Apollinaire opened the door. She was in her bathrobe and scarlet as a crayfish. She wedged the door with her foot. "We've been in bed since Sunday. We've caught the flu. Don't come in, Cendrars!" she said. "And Guillaume," I asked. "He's black all over and isn't moving anymore. Don't come in!" I shoved Jacqueline aside and ran to Guillaume's bed. Apollinaire was lying on his back. He was blackened from head to toe and gasping for breath. Upon hearing my voice, he opened his eyes. He didn't say anything to me. Then he shut his eyes again. After some time, he turned onto his left side which left him facing the wall. I exited and ran down the steps, four-by-four again, ran to the corner bistro and telephoned a physician, Dr Capmas,[141] and told him it was extremely urgent, that Apollinaire was congested and asked him whether I shouldn't cut open his earlobes to get him to piss out a little blood pending the good doctor's arrival. He advised me strongly to do nothing and said he'd be arriving presently and that his car was in front of the door. I called Serge Jastrebzoff at his office in the Italian hospital, and begged him to warn Apollinaire's mother, whom I didn't know, and to pass on the alert to his friends that he was coming, what I meant was not only that it was serious, but that it was soon going to be all over for him. In fact, when Doctor Capmas arrived, he told me right away that he had been called too late, that he could no longer do anything for Guillaume. Jacqueline had gone back to bed. In turn, she started blackening right in front of us. So, Doctor Capmas set to taking care of her. Prior to leaving, I cast a last glance towards the kitchen where Apollinaire liked to sit at his small table, under the gambrel, *oeil-de-boeuf* window. A quill was dipped into the inkwell. On one side was the tube of Harlem oil that I had given to Guillaume on Sunday. He had carefully unfolded and creased the mediaeval prospectus.

On the other side there was a thick, ancient tome, a treatise on medicine written in Dutch. At the top of a blank sheet of paper, with the calligraphy of Guillaume, was written a title, three times underlined: MY FINAL ILLNESS. It was thus that while drafting the article that I had commissioned that Guillaume Apollinaire was seized with the first convulsion of the flu which eventually got the better of him. In spite of what I told him, he either didn't have the curiosity or the faith or the courage to drink my Harlem oil. If I were in his position and he'd given it to me, I would have downed it in one shot, even if it had poisoned me, bad luck to me! Why do you have friends, and go to so much trouble collecting them if you don't believe in them? I was pretty discouraged. I returned to the lodge of the concierge. She already knew that Apollinaire was dying. She was moaning. I got her to swallow eleven drops of Harlem oil in a bowl of milk that I had scavenged up . She let me take control. I asked her whether there weren't some errands I could run for her in the neighbourhood. She didn't need anything. So, I left…

MANOLL: And Guillaume Apollinaire died and he was buried in the manner that you just related?

CENDRARS: Hold on a second, I'm not at the end of my 15 day jaunt. Apollinaire died on Saturday the 9th, during the evening. He was buried on Wednesday the 13th.[142] And Dr Capmas' streak of bad luck wasn't at an end. Several years later, in 1923, he was called again too late – this time to the death bed of Raymond Radiguet. He was the physician for **La Sirène**, a man who had a way with words, a man who had ideas, a disciple of Quinton. He would administer injections of seawater. One of his practices was to administer salt injections into the buttocks. These invigorating injections were so successful that soon everybody fashionable in Paris would show up between 5 and 7 pm in his waiting room, *rue Saint-Philippe-du Roule*. Cocteau used to say: "It's the last salon where people can actually still converse". I said to Jules Romains during a gala premiere evening: "Dr Capmas should have been the mentor for Doctor Knock…" because, over the long term, I didn't believe in him anymore. Today, he is dead, but Paul Laffitte, who ran everything over at la Sirène, believed in him right up to his last day. He also wanted to make a name for himself in high society. His idea was to launch a Thermal Oceanographic Institute. *Medice, cura te ipsum*! Life is absurd, don't you think, Manoll? But, wait, I still haven't even finished the tale of my two weeks in Paris. Friday morning was a matinéé performance of poetry we were putting on. François Beronouard had organised the event at the Théâtre de l'Avenue, *rue du Colisée* to celebrate the launch of *J'ai tué.** Raymone, Greta Prozor, Pierre Bertin and his student Debiève, Marcel Herrand reading some of my writing. It was a hit, a critical success, but not a financial one. We didn't sell one single booklet. The matinée concluded with sales of o francs, o centimes in the till. Seeing that we were downcast, Cocteau emptied out his wallet of any spare cash so at least we wouldn't leave empty-handed – we being Bernouard, Léger and me. My dear Jean, you'll have a lot of sins forgiven for that hundred sou coin. The price of the red ink edition with the drawings of Fernand Léger in blue ink and a stain of colour across the cover was 5 francs. Today, the booklet is worth a fortune. Sunday the 17th, I was back in Nice. My two weeks in Paris were over and done. Monday morning I was back at work. "Quiet, and roll 'em!" I shouted into my megaphone "Light!…" I won't dwell anymore on the steady march of time, except to say in passing that we didn't yell "Sound" because it was the era of silent movies.

MANOLL: What film were you shooting in Nice?

CENDRARS: Tenez-vous bien, Manoll. I was playing a dead man in *les Morts qui reviennent,*** the fourth part of the immortal film of Abel Gance, *J'accuse*[143] which we were completing. It was the end.

MANOLL: What you, Cendrars, an actor?

CENDRARS: My dear friend, in *J'accuse*, I did just about everything: errand boy, props handler, electrician, pyro-technician, costume designer, assistant camera-man, co-director, chauffeur for the boss, accountant, cashier and in *Return of the Dead*, I was a stiff for the photo shoots, coated in horse hemoglobin, because they had to shoot a scene where I lost my arm for a second time. I'm sure you

---

* *I have killed*
** *Return of the Dead*

know the song:

> *When Jean-Renaud went off to war*
> *Guts in his hand and not much more*

MANOLL: *Alors, ça, c'est du cinéma*!

Explanatory Notes

The text of this small volume, Blaise Cendrars speaks… is based on remarks I made during the series of Interviews produced by *Radiodiffusion française** under the title *En bourlinguant avec Blaise Cendrars.*** Because this is now being published and sold in bookshops, I changed the title so as to avoid confusion with an earlier published work: *Bourlinguer.****

These interviews were recorded from 14 to 25 April, 1950 by Michel Manoll, who had the original idea for these interviews. The recording presented no particular difficulty, save and except a few minor discords between Manoll and myself when I didn't wish to respond to certain questions that I considered to be far too indiscreet, and when I had the impression I was sitting in front of an investigating judge, or when Manoll wanted to force me into contradictions with myself, which is a characteristic fixation of interviewers.

The recording took place between April 29 and May 31 and was produced by Albert Riéra, the Ace of the broadcasting world, but nearly resulted in disaster because I was so enthused by the entire process that reminded me of film-making and its prodigious possibilities that I began cropping, cutting and deleting run-on dialogue, repetitions and literary digressions in favour of spontaneity and improvisation of dialogue. With the thirty-eight reels that we developed, Manoll and I only managed to extract thirteen interviews as compared with the fifteen initially contemplated. The cutting was a bit on the heavy side, and I take full responsibility for that.

These thirteen interviews were broadcast on the National Broadcaster between October 15 and December 15, 1950.[144]

---

* French Broadcoasting Corporation
** Vagabonding with Blaise Cendrars
*** Vagabonding

The text I am publishing today was written based on the spoken text that I had great difficulty in recovering due to the inexperience of the steno-typist provided to me. It was very difficult to achieve an exact synchronisation between two modes of mechanical reproduction, one auditory and the other spoken. But, I was able to reconstruct virtually the entire text based on my recall, supplemented by certain director's cuts in my possession and fragments of film of varying lengths.

I cut three interviews that were redundant. I took advantage of the opportunity to rework the scenes and to reverse the order of output. I completely revised the interview on the death of Apollinaire. Anything that was not in the interest of the written form, so as to get closer to the original text. Alas! We don't have audio-books yet, so the voice is missing, the voice of the microphone…

Poor poets, let's get to work.

Paris, February 29, 1952

Post-scriptum

I wanted to dedicate this book to you, my dear Paul Gibson,[145] but because you hold such a high position within *Radiodiffusion Française*, I refrained from doing so, fearful that I would be accused of being a toadying sycophant. After reflection and seeing nobody else anywhere as worthy as you, my fine Paul, I dedicate the volume to you anyways, so take it, it's yours. I offer it as a souvenir of our meeting in Blois and to commemmorate our own coverage of those nights of the exodus, during June 1940, rattling about inside your oversized aluminium Radio truck, and me, disguised as an Englishman. Tibi.

BLAISE

Endnotes

INTERVIEW I

[1] Michel Manoll (1911-1984), the interviewer, is the author of numerous collections of poetry (*La Première Chance, Goutte d'ombre, Incarnada*) and of poetic art (*L'été andalousien*, 1981). He was a member of the Rochefort school, comprised of followers of René-Guy Cadou, including Luc Bérimont, Jean Bouhier and Jean Rousselot. Cendrars was one of their references as an author.

Albert Riéra (1895-1968), the producer of the original interviews for French television, was the cousin of the film director Jean Vigo with whom he worked as an assistant director for *Zéro de conduite* (1933) and *l'Atalante* (1934) and with whom he co-wrote the dialogues of this last film. Was it during this time period that he met Cendrars? The poet had written the scenario for *Contrebandiers* that was abandoned due to the death of Vigo (TADA 13). Riéra subsequently became the "ace of the radio waves" as admired by Cendrars and with whom he frequently collaborated in the RTF of Paul Gilson, in particular for *Films sans images*. He was also a visual artist, and produced the sketch of Cendrars that appears on the cover page of Henry Miller's *Blaise Cendrars* (Denoel, 1951).

[2] 96th replaces 67th in the personal copy of Cendrars.

[3] Note added by Cendrars in his personal copy.

[4] Sonia Delaunay confirms that this initial meeting took place at Apollinaire's home, 202, boulevard Saint-Germain. During one of the Wednesdays when the poet received his friends, she saw "seated on a grand divan, a young, small, frail, blond-haired boy." Invited to the Delaunay studio, 3, rue des Grands-Augustins, Cendrars arrived the following day with *Les Pâques* (Easter in New York), a poem that Sonia greeted with enthusiasm,

and inspired her in her creation of a cover made of papers affixed to chamois skin. "Since that day, Cendrars has become our best friend" (*Nous irons jusqu'au soleil,* op.cit. p. 53-54.)

[5] Towards the end of June 1914, the "simultaneous" controversy ignited, opposing Cendrars, then Apollinaire against the Poet Henri-Martin Barzun, Director of the review Poem and Drama, who claimed he was the inventor of *simultanéisme* and Orphism. Cendrars used the name Barzum, a character of Souvestre and Allain's *Fantômas,* to ridicule his poem "Fantômas" which he used at that time in bad faith to challenge the right to use the word "simultaneous" in the Prose of the Transsiberian (Nineteen elastic poems, 1919, TADA1, p. 87-88).

[6] Cendrars met Guillaume Apollinaire in 1912, undoubtedly in November, and he maintained with him a distrustful friendship and frequently conflictual rivalry. The dispute between the two poets probably crystallized around the alleged influence of "Pâques" on "Zone", resurrected as a contemporary issue by Robert Goffin in *Entrer en poésie* (1948). While he refused to explicitly remark on the issue, Cendrars openly implied, as in this interview, that for him, the question – or the wound – remained an open one. See Pierre Caizergues, *"Cendrars et Apollinaire",* Sud, issue on Cendrars, 1988, p. 71-102.

[7] Hanns Heinz Ewers (1871-1941) German novelist influenced by Edgar Poe, is the author of *Mandragore* (1911), and of *Vampire* (1921). He compromised himself by adhering to Nazism. Cendrars' reading during his youth led him to borrow two titles: Moganni Nameh and Blauwe Indianer ("The Blue Indians", chapter *n* of *Moravagine*). He ironically referred to a title of Ewers, *Les Indes et moi* (1911), in *Sous le signe de François Villon* (TADA 11, p. 180).

[8] Cendrars appears to be confusing the two journeys made by Robert Delaunay to Berlin during 1913. During January, in the company of Apollinaire, Delaunay attended the opening of the monograph exhibition devoted to him by the Der Strum gallery, linked with the review of the same name directed by Herwarth Walden. The exhibition presented the series of "Windows" and an album published on this occasion opens on "The Windows" of Apollinaire who also, during his sojourn, two conferences on Rude and on *Les Commencements du Cubisme.* Several months later, Robert Delaunay returned to Berlin in the company of Sonia and Cendrars, but without Apollinaire, on the occasion of the first German

Autumn Fair organized by the review Der Sturm, from September 20 to December 1, 1913. On this occasion, a layout of the "Prose of the Transsiberian" was displayed that would be published several weeks later. The presence of Cendrars at the Autumn Fair is also evidenced by a telegram to Walden, on September 30, reporting a set-to with him that broke out during the sojourn. It was only in March that Walden met Cendrars when he travelled to Paris in order to prepare the Autumn Fair with the Delaunays.

[9] In 1914, Apollinaire published three volumes at Briffaut in the collection "*L'Histoire Romanesque*", Rome of the Borgias, The End of Babylon and The Three Don Juans. The first is "nearly entirely the work of René Dalize" according to Michel Décaudin who excluded it from his edition of *Oeuvres en prose* in "La Pléiade" (Gallimard, I, 1977, p. 1410-1412). The two others multiplied their borrowings and it is not therefore to be excluded that Cendrars may have had his hand in *La Fin de Babylone*. René Dalize (1879-1914), the pen name of René Dupuy, was the condisciple of Apollinaire at the Saint-Charles de Monaco. Naval officer, he interrupted his career in 1907 to write. He was one of the founders of the review Les Soirées de Paris. He fell in combat nearby Craonne, on May 7, 1917. André Billy (1882-1971), journalist and writer, met Apollinaire in 1903. By 1910, they had become friends. He also was a co-founder of Les Soirées de Paris.

[10] *Les Hommes Nouveaux* (New Men) was the name given by Cendrars and his Hungarian friend Emile Szittya (1886-1964) to the Franco-German publishing house and free review they created in 1912 in Paris. The review followed up on the review Neue Menschen that Szittya had published in Paris in 1910-1911. Easter in New York first appeared in Les Hommes Nouveau, as did Séquences and the Prose of the Transsibérien et de la petite Jeanne de France the following year. Knowledge of this period remained obscure for a long period of time, and was rekindled by Christine Le Quellec Cottier in *Devenir Cendrars* (Champion, 2004, p. 179-195).

[11] Cendrars personally knew Victor Serge (1890-1947), aka Viktor Lvovitch Kibaltchiche, French-speaking revolutionary and writer. Born in Brussels of Russian parents in exile, Serge frequented libertarian circles from a young age and his sympathies for the Bonnot gang led to a five year prison sentence in 1912. He relocated in Russia and became a member of the Communist Party, but was expelled in 1928, and in 1933 deported by Stalin to Siberia. He was freed following an international

campaign and banished. He died in Mexico in 1947. Editor at the journal l'Anarchie (1909-1912), he was the author of an abundant work, particularly novels (The Toulaev Affair, 1948, that Cendrars cites in *Le Lotissement du Ciel* (Sky), TADA 12, p. 311), as well as the *Memoirs of a revolutionary* 1901-1941 (1951).

[12] Jules Joseph Bonnot and his group of anarchists called the "Bonnot gang", sowed terror in the Parisian region, practicing a form of attack on banks hitherto unknown in France, the automobile hold-up, between December 21, 1911 (robbery of rue Ordener) and on April 21, 1912. That day, in Choisy-le-Roi, "with three companies of the Republican Guard, and two infantry batallions, all the personnel of the Tour pointue, without forgetting pretty well every shooting organisation within a ten league perimeter, and after having used several quintaux of dynamite to blow up the garage, the forces of order finally succeeding in bringing the outlaw to heel" (*Le Crapouillot* cited by André Salmon, La Terreur noire, Volume 2, 10/18, 1973, p. 242). Bonnot and Dubois were dead. The remainder of the gang was arrested on May 14, 1912 in Noegent-sur-Marne. Following the trial, Raymond Callemin aka Raymond la Science, Monier aka Séménoff and Soudy were sentenced to death and had their heads cut off on boulevard Arago, on April 23, 1913. Cendrars gave the nickname of Raymond la Science to the psychiatrist who assisted Moravagine in his escape and recounted his exploits.

[13] Marius Hanot signed a highly complimentary article on "André Suarès" in October 1912 in the sole and rare issue of the review *Les Hommes nouveaux*. No information is available on this friend of Cendrars and Szittya other than the fact that he actually existed. The response of Cendrars to Manoll leads to the conclusion that he wrote this paper himself and the writing of the text would appear to support the plausibility of this. Furthermore, we know that Cendrars contributed to this issue under at least three different names : Blaise Cendrars, Jack Lee and Diogenes. André Suarès (1868-1948) was for a long time considered the equal of Claudel, Gide or Valéry prior to falling into obscurity. This praise of the author of *Voyage du Condottière* by Cendrars is unique.

[14] The poet Louis de Gonzague Frick (1883-1958) was a great friend of Apollinaire and Max Jacob, but also of the surrealists (Breton, Desnos) who all held him in high esteem. Wearing a monocle, he was known as a dandy with a fine sense of humour. He moved in 1935 to *rue du Lunain*. He founded as the School of Lunain as a lark, participated in by Michel

Manoll and other poets of the future School of Rochefort ad he published a review, Le Lunain. On this poet, since fallen into obscurity, Sarane Alexandrian published a study, followed by an anthology of his texts and letters, in the review *Eupérieus inconnue* (no 20, January-March 2001).

[15] Antoinette appears in the *"Première rhapsodie gitane"* (TADA 5, p. 18%7-210). She left Cendrars for Marthe, the disfigured woman of Gustave Lerouge.

[16] On the caravan of misery of Father François, see *L'Homme Foudroyé*, (TADA 5, p. 193-196).

INTERVIEW II

Most of this interview is drawn from the thirteenth and final radio interview.

[17] No evidence supports this sojourn of the Sauser family into Egypt, that forms part of the legend of the poet. Heliopolis is the mythical land of the phoenix where Blaise Cendrars, under his pseudonym, imagined himself as fowler. The most extensive portrait of Georges Sauser (1851-1927), the unhappy inventor who was scorned by his wife, can be found in *Vol à Voile* (1932;TADA).

[18] The coat-of-arms of the Sauser family can be found in the church at Sigriswil, a village of the Bernese Oberland. This is where Cendrars married Raymone on October 27, 1949.

[19] Coronel Luiz Logrado is the hero of "Boa", one of the Brazilian tales published in *"Mes chasses"* (*D'Outremer à Indigo*), 1940; TADA 8, p. 371-390). A man from another era, possessed by the demon of hunting, he eventually was the victim of the sucuruju (Anaconda), a boa constrictor that he considered as the personal enemy of his family.

[20] In 1913, Cendrars copied the *Très plaisante et recreative hystoire du très preulx et vaillant chevallier Perceval le Galloys jadis chevallier de la Table Ronde le quel acheva les adventures de Sainct Graal, au temps du noble Roy Arthus* for Apollinaire. Due to the war, the volume was only released in

1918 in the « *Nouvelle Bibliothèque Bleue* » of Librairie Payot in Paris, with the notice "published by Guillaume Apollinaire" to which Cendrars added in his own handwriting "and Blaise Cendrars" on the copy he forwarded "to Blaise Cendrars: his friend/Guil. Apollinaire"...(ALS Berne).

[21] Pierre-Paul Plan (1870-1951) is the author of a *Bibliographie rabelaisienne* (1904), of *Jean-Jacques et Malesherbes* (1912), of *Jacques Callot Graveur* (1914). He challenged Pierre Louys who claimed that the plays of Molière had been written by Corneille (*Mercure de France*, December 15, 1919). At Payot, he directed the "Petite collection romantique" and the "Nouvelle Bibliothèque Bleue". His name does not appear on Perceval le Galloys.

[22] "Paris, Port-de-Mer", final part of *Bourlinguer,* is wholly devoted to a paradoxical eulogy to the act of reading as taking a drug (1948 : TADA 9, p. 317-421).

[23] Charles Chadenat ((1859-1938) directed the bookstore Americana for fifty years, from 1888 to 1938. Cendrars evokes his memory at length in "*Paris, Port-de-Mer*" (*Bourlinguer,* TADA 9, p. 346-362). His son interpreted this admiring portrait to be a cruel caricature which triggered a polemic. He even demanded a retraction, which Cendrars refused to sign.

[24] During early 1948, Cendrars left Aix-en-Provence, where he had resided since the 1940 debacle, to take up quarters at Villefranche-sur-Mer, initially at the Clair Logis, avenue Estève, then, from April onwards, in Saint-Ségond. This property had an immense terrace where Robert Doisneau took numerous photographs of the poet. This is where Cendrars completed *Sky* on May 1, 1940, and where he wrote *La Banlieue de Paris* (Paris Suburb). He left Villefranche during Spring 1950, subsequently returning to Paris, initially at 100, boulevard Port-Royal (5th) where he resided when he recorded his interviews with Manoll, but during their broadcast, he had already moved to 23, rue Jean-Dolent (XIVth) opposite La Santé prison.

[25] The "fieldstone house" of Cendrars at Tremblay-sur-Mauldre, nearby Versailles, was pillaged during the Second World War. In December 1950, he announced to Paul Gilson that he had "miraculously discovered most of his personal library in the shop of an antique dealer in Biarritz, including a chest of manuscripts". (Paul Gilson, *Hommage et contribution bio-bibliographique,* F.J. Temple editors, Lausanne, Le Front littéraire, 1983, p.

40). These archives are the basis of the Fonds Balide-Cendrars conserved today at the Swiss literary Archives in Berne.

[26] The tale of this celebrated and just as imaginary fugue took place in *Vol à voile* (1932, TADA 9, p. 435-470).

[27] Manoll is alluding to a passage from "Genoa" where Cendrars declared that he divided his life "into two phases" (*Bourlinguer*, 1948; TADA 9, p. 193).

[28] This statement is surprising: *La Vie Dangereuse*, second volume of "*Histoires Vraies*" [True Tales] includes "*J'ai saigné*" (I bled) one of the major autobiographical texts of Cendrars (Grasset, 1938; TADA 11, p. 24).

[29] *Eloge de la vie dangereuse* [In Praise of the Dangerous Life]was published in a limited edition booklet by *Editeurs réunis* in 1926, then republished in *Aujourd'hui* (1931; TADA 11, p. 24).

[30] Tiradentes, small colonial city of the Sate of Minas Gerais, owes its name to a 19th century revolutionary, José da Silva Xavier, aka Tiradentes "the tooth-ripper" who sought the declaration of the republic and the abolition of slavery. He was hung and quartered in Rio in 1792.

[31] In "Fébronio (Magia Sexualis)", Cendrars tells the story of this fanatical Brazilian assassin, who in 1927, terrorised the population of Rio by his serial murders. Quickly arrested, he spent the rest of his life in prison where he died in his eighties (he appeared in a documentary shot in 1981). Did Cendrars meet him in his prison? Nothing proves that. The interview that he claims to have had with Fébronio appears to owe more to his reading of the Brazilians, particularly the specialized medical press. The author of *Moravagine* clearly saw in him a reincarnation of his diabolical alter ego (*La Vie Dangereuse*, 1938; TADA 8, p. 223-260).

[32] After three years of silence in Aix-en-Provence, Cendrars returned to writing in 1943, with the intention of writing *La Carissima*. Little by little, *L'Homme Foudroyé* – under the sign of Lazarus, the brother of Mary Magdalen – would replace this initial project which never reached fruition. The few fragments remaining were published by Anna Maibach at Champion in 1996.

[33] This list of 3000 words has never been found, and would have positioned Cendrars by the use of this arbitrary, formal constraint[5], as a descendant

of the great *rhétoriqueurs* and a cousin of the *oulipists* of Raymond Queneau. On the other hand, numerous work sheets disclose that the imagination of Cendrars was stimulated by lists of words, names, chapters or works to be undertaken.

[34] This conference constituted the VIIIth section of *Aujourd'hui*, titled "Poets" (TADA 11, p. 87-114) These stenographic notes of "someone in attendance" are dated February 21, 1924. Cendrars also gave a conference "On Black Literature" on May 29, 1924 in Sao Paulo and repeated the experience on June 10, 1925 in Madrid. This hitherto unpublished conference was released by Christine le Quellec Cottier (TADA 10, p. 471-488).

[35] Fragments of *Au coeur du monde* were published by Cendrars between 1919 and 1944. The discovery of a working manuscript revealed other unpublished fragments, but leave an impression that the poem remains incomplete. (TADA 10, p. 127-136, 377-381).

[36] EO: "mentales", corrected by Cendrars on his personal copy. Kodak (Documentary) was published by Stock in 1924. As the firm Kodak protested against the use of its name, Cendrars rebaptized his collection Documentaries when he included it in his *Poésies Complètes* in 1944. We now know that most of these "verbal photographs" come by way of collage from the serial novel authored by Gustave Lerouge, *The Mysterious Doctor Cornelius* (TADA 1, p. 139 -176 and 382-397).

[37] *Feuilles de route* [Roadmaps]I. Formosa is the last collection of poems published by Cendrars, that included under this title a series of seven *plaquettes* (booklets), but he quickly abandoned the idea. The "postal cards" written during this final trip to Brazil are mixed in with the collages (1924; TADA 1, p. 177- 252 and 388-397).

[38] This was the night of September 1, 1917 – the night he turned thirty – during the course of which Cendrars says he wrote in a single sitting *La Fin du monde filmée par l'Ange N.-D.* at La Pierre, nearby Méréville. He told the tale of this nocturnal epiphany on three separate occasions l (*Moravagine*, TADA 7, p. 236; *Le Sans-Nom,* TADA 5, p. 393-395; *L'Homme Foudroyé*, TADA 5, p. 232))

INTERVIEW III

Interview III is a reworked version of the first radio interview.

[39] Abbot Jacques Paul Migne (1800-1875), a Balzacian character, is the author of an unprecedented body of editorial work. In 1836, he founded the Petit-Montrouge publishing house (where he published the writings of the Fathers of the Church in a monumental Greek and Latin *Patrology*, which was widely popular. Jacques Roubaud refers to the 366 volumes in *La Belle Hortense* (Seghers, 1990, p. 250).

[40] Igor Stravinsky (1882-1971) and Cendrars met and became friends at the home of their mutual friend Eugenia Errazuriz, Grande dame from Chile and patron of the arts who received "her" musician and "her poet" notably in Biarritz. ("her" painter was Picasso). Their correspondence on the topic of *Ragtime*, a score of the musician that Cendrars wished to reproduce in *La Sirène* in 1918, was published in "Continent Cendrars" (no 10, Champion, 1995-1996, p. 141-171, presentation of Jean-Carlo Fluckiger).

[41] The two volumes of this novel, *Le Plan de l'Aiguille* (to which Cendrars alludes in his response) and *The Confessions of Dan Yack*, appeared in *Au Sans Pareil*, in 1929. In 1946, Cendrars reworked them and merged them into a single volume in the short-lived *Editions de la Tour*. This last version was the one that was republished in TADA 4.

[42] Louis Parrot, Blaise Cendrars, Seghers, « *Poètes d'aujourd'hui*, no 11, 1948, p. 51. Poet, novelist, journalist, L. Parrot (1906-1948) recounted his life in the French Resistance in *L'Intelligence en guerre* ((1945). In the collection «*Poètes d'aujourd'hui* », he also published essays on Eluard (1944) and Lorca (1947) who were among his friends. *The Adventures of Arthur Gordon Pym* (1838) is a tale by Edgar Allan Poe, translated by Baudelaire in 1857.

[43] The review *La Rose Rouge*, directed by Maurice Magre and Pierre Silvestre, published only sixteen issues between May 3 and August 14, 1919. It adopted as its motto "Against besotted thought, literary routine, we shall defend with all our energy, without hatred or bias, without indulgent cronyism, what is beautiful, young and human." Its directing mind was Jean Galmot, the businessman and member of the Guyana Parliament.

Cendrars wrote his biography in *Rhum* (1930). As a regular contributor to this review, Cendrars wrote nine columns under the title "*Modernités*" – eight on painting and one on cinema (no 7) -, as well as three *contes nègres* [negro tales](no 4) that were reprinted in his *Anthologie Nègre* (1921), a "Short Stendhalian column" (no 6, never reprinted) and a republication of "Easter in New York" with numerous variants (no 14). The fact that "*Modernités*" was written by a poet who was neither a collector nor a regular columnist can no doubt be explained as a discreet settling of accounts with painters and art dealers at the instigation of Léger who was then taking his distance from the cubists ((see Christian Derouet, "*Blaise Cendrars et 'l'Effort Moderne'*", in *Cendrars le bourlingueur des deux rives*, A. Colin, 1995, p 65-73)When he reprinted his "*Modernités*" in *Aujourd'hui*, Cendrars followed them up with an epilogue: "*Pour prendre congé des peintres*" ["So long to the painters"], the title of which evokes its underlying intent; (TADA 5, p. 173)

44 *Pauvre Lélian* : reference to Paul Verlaine who coined the nickname by an anagram of his actual name.

45 Allusion to *L'Homme Foudroyé* (The Shattered Man), where the poet describes this rupture with the Parisian literary world and the stashing away of *Au coeur du monde*, nailed shut in a softwood chest, at the origin of the "reckoning" of his life as a man" (TADA 5, p. 173).

46 "*Quand on aime, il faut partir*": version slightly reworked of "Quand tu aimes, il faut partir", first verse of the poem "*Tu es plus belle que le ciel et la mer*" (*Feuilles de route*, 1924; TADA 1, p. 184. See also *L'Homme Foudroyé*, TADA 5, p. 131).

47 André Gide was the target of a cruel jibe in *L'Homme Foudroyé*, (1945) TADA 5, p.234).

48 "Flanchard" (Coward) replaced "vaseux" (clay-footed) on the typed MS for printing. Philippe Soupault (1897-1990) co-wrote *Les Champs Magnétiques* with André Breton, a text of automatist writing that marked the birth of the surrealist experiment. In 1926, he broke off from the group while remaining faithful to his original principles. Cendrars' acrimonious judgment of a poet who was one of his friends at the end of World War One is surprising, given that he had frequently expressed notable admiration for his elder, in his poem "Westwego" (1922) and in numerous interviews. This passage deeply hurt Soupault.

⁴⁹ After several attempts to approach Cendrars by the younger man, the relations between Cendrars and André Breton (1896-1966) oscillated between distrust and hostility. Among other things, a rivalry in the conception of the modern after the death of Apollinaire, the rejection by Cendrars of any avant-garde collective articulated through a political project, and a patent personality conflict all contributed to their bad relations.

⁵⁰ Louis Aragon (1897-1982) was one of the founders of the surrealist movement. He broke with the movement in 1932 in favour of the French Communist Party. In the modern poetry conference Cendrars organised in Brazil in 1924, he cited and commented on "*Lever*" a poem from *Feu de joie* in (1920) (TADA 11, p. 99-104).

⁵¹ In his 1924 Brazil conference, Cendrars also brought Robert Desnos (1900-1945) into the public eye, citing him and commenting on a poem "*Corps et biens*" (1930), "*Elégant cantique de Salomé Salomon*" (TADA 11, p. 106-107). In the same vein of popular poetry, it is remarkable that Cendrars almost never refers to Jacques Prévert, the other poet of Robert Doisneau.

⁵² Cendrars developed this eulogy in *Sous le signe de François Villon* [Under the sign of François Villon], an essay written in 1939 and published in 1952 (TADA 11, p. 15-182).

⁵³ Citation of Paul Verlaine: "No. This century was Gallican and Jansenist!/It is towards the Middle Ages, enormous and delicate/ that my broken heart must navigate/Far from our days of carnal spirit and sad flesh" (*Sagesse*, I, IX, in *Oeuvres poétiques complètes*, Editor J. Borel, Gallimard, "Bibliothèque de la Pléiade", 1962, p. 249).

INTERVIEW IV

Interview IV is a reworked version of the second radio interview.

⁵⁴ Cendrars always referred to *Aurélia* (1955) by its subtitle *Le Rêve et la vie*. *Dichtung und Wahrheit* (Poetry and Truth) is the title given by Goethe (1749-1832) to his autobiography.

55 In one of his Notes addressed to the unknown Reader, following "Genoa", Cendrars cites the second quatrain of de Nerval's sonnet, "*El Desdichado*" as one of the "secret keys" to his tale (TADA 9, p. 256, note j.)

56 Along with Rémy de Gourmont and François Villon, Gérard de Nerval (1808-1855) was a literary mentor and touchstone for Cendrars throughout his life. He appropriated the formula "*Je suis l'autre*" [I am the other] written by Nerval at the bottom of one of his final portraits by Gervais. Freddy Sauser inserted it at the bottom of a self-portrait drawn in New York on "5May 1912", when he was preparing to change his name. The formula returns as a leitmotif for Cendrars like a motto where the fascination for the double mixes in with a desire for metamorphosis.

57 No conserved document confirms this project of a triptych; *Negro Anthology* was only published at *Editions de la Sirène* in 1921, then by *Au Sans Pareil* in 1927 and by Corréa in 1947. Cendrars subsequently published two other collections of *Negro Tales* and wrote the ballet booklet *La Création du Monde*, in 1923. All these texts were republished in TADA 11.

58 Darius Milhaud (1892-1974) was part of the Group of Six with Georges Auric, Louis Durey, Arthur Honegger, Francis Poulenc and Germaine Tailleferre. In 1917, he accompanied Paul Claudel, whom he served as a secretary, to Brazil. This inspired his composition *Le Boeuf sur le toit*. Subsequently, after returning from the United States, he composed a jazz-influenced symphony work for the ballet *La Création du Monde* (1923)on a booklet of Cendrars.

59 In "*Le Cercle du Diamant*", (*Histoires vraies*, 1937; TADA 8, p. 55), Cendrars had already mentioned Donga, whose real name was Ernesto Joaquim Maria dos Santos (1891-1974). Composer of the first recorded samba, this famous Brazilian musician toured France in 1922, with the group Os oito batutas.

60 *L'Homme Foudroyé* (1945), *La Main Coupée* (1946), *Bourlinguer* (1948) and *Le Lotissement du Ciel* (1949) were all published by Denoel under the same indigo blue cover.

61 Cendrars describes these principles of composition in *Bourlinguer* (TADA 9, p. 193-195).

62 *L'Avocat du diable* and *Les Paradis enfantins* are probably the books that

Cendrars was happy enough just to fantasize about, contrary to *La Caris-sima*, the failure of which left him bitter.

[63] *Emmène-moi au bout du monde!*...was released in January 1956, after a lengthy labour that was costly to Cendrars and left him exhausted. The following summer, he fell victim to his first stroke. (TADA 14).

[64] *L'Homme Foudroyé* (TADA 5, p. 89-90, 101 note b).

INTERVIEW V

Interview V is a reworked and rewritten version of the fourth radio interview.

[65] René Rouveret, a former sailor according to Cendrars, illustrated the deluxe edition of *Vieux-Port*, published by Jean Vigneau in 1946. Various setbacks meant that this pre-original edition of a part of *L'Homme Foudroyé* was published after its republication in the original edition by Denoel (TADA 5, p. 43, with two Rouveret lithographs).

[66] Sigriswil. See supra note 4.

[67] "*Le Panama ou les aventures de mes sept oncles*" (*Poésies complètes*; TADA 1, p. 41). Completed in 1914, the poem was only published in 1918 by Editions de la Sirène.

[68] A calculated confession: Martin Birmann, who appears in *Gold* as the tutor of the Suter children, is also and especially the author of the biography of Suter that Cendrars used to write his novel at the end of 1924. Pastor, Member of Parliament, state councillor, protector of abandoned children and the poor, Birmann (1828-1890) was a friend of Suter who supervised the education of the children of the fugitive. The general was his testamentary executor (TADA 2, p xv, 87-88, 100-107).

[69] On the genesis of *Gold*, the corrections and the alterations made for his new edition, and the ins and outs of the Trenker trial, see Claude Leroy, *L'Or de Blaise Cendrars*, in the collection "Foliothèque" of Gallimard (1991).

[70] One of the poems of *Feuilles de Route*, "Pernambuco", attributes this top-ographical fantasy to Victor Hugo: "Victor Hugo calls it Fernandbouc of the Blue Mountains/And an old author I'm reading calls it Ferdinand-bourg of the thousand Churches/ In Indian this name means the Forked Mouth" (TADA 1, p. 245). Cendrars returns to the topic at length in "*L'Amiral*", accompanying his text with etymological considerations (*D'Outremer à Indigo*, TADA 8, p. 395-397). But this reference is approx-imative. It doesn't come from a poem but from Ruy Blas, whose hero rages against "ministers of integrity" who sell off Spanish possessions: Every-thing is gone – We have, since Philippe IV/ Lost Portugal, Brazil, without fighting; […] and Fernambouc, and the Blue Mountains!" (III 2); The Blue Mountains are located in Jamaica (Victor Hugo, *Complete Works*, Ed. Jean Massin, Le Club Français du livre, 1967, V, p. 724).

[71] Allusion to the new "*Le crocodile*" in "*Mes chasses*" (*D'Oultremer à In-digo*, 1940; TADA 8, p. 354-371).

[72] *L'Homme Foudroyé* (TADA 5, p. 245-248).

[73] The ibadou or ipadu, from the tupi ipaʾdu, is an evergreen shrub that possesses the same properties as coca in less potent forms. Cendrars had already celebrated its properties and virtues in "*En transatlantique dans la forêt vierge*" (*Histoires vraies*, TADA8, p. 155) then in *Sky*, book to the glory of levitation ("The new patron saint of aviation", p. 63-68).

[74] Incipit and refrain from an untitled poem republished in *Vers nouveaux et chansons* in Arthur Rimbaud, Complete Works (ed. Antoine Adam), Gallimard, "la Pléiade", 1972, p. 88-89). The relationship of Cendrars with Rimbaud (1854-1891) escapes easy definition. In *Sous le signe de François Villon*, he ironically commented on the contradictory, but in his eyes abu-sive, interpretations of the work and the life of Rimbaud to finally con-clude: "Rimbaud silenced his own voice. It is the sole thing with which he can be reproached and it is my sole reproach of him. A man of strength forgets his past; He should have returned, remained silent or taken up writing anew, but in an entirely new direction." This passage suggests a parallel between the destiny of Rimbaud and that of Cendrars, who emerged from silence and his injury to write – using his left hand – some-thing entirely different".

[75] In *Une Nuit dans la forêt,* in 1929, Cendrars announced *Notre pain quo-tidien* as a « great novel in several volumes » : « something that, in my

mind, is the equivalent of Victor Hugo's *Les Misérables*, but *les misérables* of my work will not be a single social class, but all social classes. I would like to recount how people earn their bread, their daily bread" (TADA 3, p. 174-175). He referred to this again in *L'Homme Foudroyé* (1945; TADA 5, p. 274-276) and in *Trop c'est trop* (TADA 11, p. 462). This projects which curiously prefigures *La Vie mode d'emploi* of Georges Perec appears to be limited to a few notes in the abundant phantom library of Cendrars.

[76] Cendrars mentions for the first time *La Vie et la mort du Soldat inconnu* upon his return from Brazil in 1928 and he worked there intermittently up until 1933; Only two excerpts would appear in reviews, bu the novel was not destroyed: it remained unfinished. All the surviving unpublished fragments were pubished by Champion (Ed. Judith Trachsel, 1995).

[77] This passage cites, almost word for word, a text published in *La Gazette des Lettres* (June 15, 1951), "The novel that I will never write", that would be published in *Trop c'est trop* (1957; TADA 11, p. 461-463).

[78] *Prose du Transsibérien et de la petite Jeanne de France* (1913; TADA 1, p. 19-20).

INTERVIEW VI

Interview VI is a reworked version of the eighth radio interview.

[79] The Russian painter Marc Chagall (1887-1985) moved to Paris in 1912. In *My Life*, he recounts how he became a friend of Cendrars who visited him in his atelier at La Ruche (see following note). The poet evokes his "demented canvasses" in the *prose du Transsibérien* and he dedicated the 4th of the Nineteen Elastic Poems and a prose poem "La Pitié" (Les Soirées de Paris, No 25, June 15, 1914; TADA 1, 321; republished in Aujourd'hui, TADA 11, p. 73). A certified portrait of the poet by the painter is unfortunately lost.

[80] La Ruche was a cité of artistes located at 2, passage de Dantzig, in the XVth arrondissement of Paris, nearby the Vaugirard slaughterhouses (since demolished). It was founded in 1902 by the sculptor Alfred Boucher in a rotunda that was built during the recently-held Universal (World) Ex-

hibition. By welcoming in her "honeycomb, among other 'bees' Léger, Chagall, Kisling, Modigliani, Soutine, Csaky, Zadkine, Archipenko" she was the crucible of the School of Paris" (Jeanine Warnod, *La Ruche & Montparnasse*, Weber, 1978).

[81] Cendrars undoubtedly met Amedeo Modigliani (1884-1920) in La Ruche, prior to the Great War. The painter left behind a dozen portraits (drawings and paintings) of his poet friend. One of them was used as a frontispiece for Nineteen elastic poems (1919). Cendrars wrote a poem "On a portrait of Modigliani" (TADA 1, 94) and described their promenades and drinking bouts in "Genoa" (*Bourlinguer*, TADA 9, p. 209-211).

[82] Cendrars met Fernand Léger at the opening exhibition of the *Salon de la Section d'Or*, at La Boetie gallery, on October 10, 1912, according to Miriam Cendrars. The experience of the war created a close friendship between the two.

[83] This is the thirteenth of the "Nineteen elastic poems", dated "February 1914" (TADA 1, p. 85)

[84] Ambroise Vollard (1868-1939) art dealer and owner of a gallery at 6, rue Lafitte, that was a famous meeting place during the years preceding the Great War. His *Souvenirs d'un marchand de tableaux,* published in 1937, described his visit to Cendrars in Tremblay-sur-Mauldre; "Everything grows marvellously here. Why don't you come, Vollard? As a matter of fact, there is an old house surrounded by a large garden that is for sale. Come and we'll go see it!" (reprint, Albin Michel, 1989, p. 393-394). In *Bourlinguer*, Vollard was described as being "tethered like a membrane" to each of his canvasses (TADA 9, p. 411-412).

[85] Sawo is a key character of *"Rhapsodies Gitanes"* (*L'Homme Foudroyé*, TADA 5) who also appears in *La Main Coupée* (TADA 6). He is the son of the gypsy mother whose tribe welcomed Cendrars in the wake of the Great War, in the south of Paris. On a letter sent by a certain Bravo, Cendrars noted, on July 19, on a signed apostille stamp: "this Bravo is the Sawo of the 'Rhapsodie' and who appears at the beginning of *L'Homme Foudroyé*". In Tzigane language cavo means "son", "boy" (Patrick Williams, "The Gitanes in the Rhapsodies Gitanes" Etudes Tsiganes 1987/3, p. 5).

[86] Cendrars spent the summer of 1917 in Courcelles, a hamlet bordering Méréville, to the south of Etampes. This sojourn marks a turning point in

the life of the amputee who discovered his new identity as a left-handed poet. He rented a room transformed into a stable in La Pierre, the neighbouring village, where he wrote in one night, *La Fin du monde filmée par l'Ange N.-D.* (see supra note 24). The watercress salt designates by metaphor the revelations intervened during this summer.

[87] "*L'Eubage, récit d'un voyage interstellaire* [The Druid, tale of an interstellar voyage] "aux antipodes de l'unité" was an order placed with Cendrars by the fashion designer/arts patron Jacques Doucet, as told in "The Night" in *Sky* (TADA 12, p. 217-222). Written for the most part in Méréville, but published solely in 1926, *L'Eubage* (transposed on the spot) recounts the traumatic experience of Cendrars during Summer 1917 (TADA 7, p. p. 285-315 and notes p. 369-378).

[88] Bikoff was in the squadron of Corporal Cendrars (*La Main Coupée*, TADA 5, p. 66-73). Cendrars attributes to him an invention that is not his: the war of 1914-1918 was in fact a war of camouflage. Lures were used to mislead expectations of the enemy, install shooting positions and to hide preparations.

INTERVIEW VII

Interview VII is a reworked version of the fifth radio interview

[89] Max Jacob (1876-1944), poet and painter, was a close friend of Picasso whom he met in 1901 and who acted as his godfather at his baptism, on February 18, 1915, under the name of Cyprien. He withdrew to Saint-Benoît-sur-Loire as of 1932, he was arrested by the Germans on February 24, 1944, and interned at the Drancy camp where he died of pulmonary congestion. His relations with Cendrars appear to have been sporadic and distant.

[90] Poet, boxer, adventurer, Fabian Lloyd, aka Arthur Cravan (1887-1920) is considered to be one of the founders of Dada. The circumstances of his disappearance remain mysterious. Cendrars described his recollections of Cravan at length and with admiration in *Sky* (TDA 12, p. 230-241).

[91] Well-known local dance hall, the *bal Bullier* was located opposite *La*

Closerie des Lilas, at the location of the current Centre universitaire Jean-Sarrailh. Moise Kisling portrayed it in one of the drawings that illustrate *Une Guerre au Luxembourg* (1916; TADA 1, p. 106).

[92] Painter and decorator of Russian origin, Sonia Delaunay (1885-1979), née Stern, was adopted by her uncle Henri Terk, whose name she adopted. She moved to Paris in 1905, entered into a convenience marriage with the collector Wilhelm Uhde and then divorced him to marry Robert Delaunay in 1912. In *Nous irons jusqu'au soleil* (Robert Laffont, 1978) she recounts the genesis of the book-canvas that would link her name with that of their great friend Cendrars. The reading of the poem inspired him with the idea of a vertical book and of a "harmony of colours that unfold simultaneously with the poem". Poet and painter jointly selected the characters the various types and sizes, "a revolutionary thing in those times". These characters had been coloured like the background of the poem so as to harmonize with the illustration. The entire presentation was introduced by the authors as the "first simultaneous book".

[93] Vladimir Mayakovsky (1893-1930), the most celebrated poet of the Russian futurist movement, was also by revolutionary conviction the author of slogans and propaganda posters. He committed suicide in 1930. Cendrars probably met him in Paris and describes him in the section "Poets" in *Aujourd'hui* 5TADA 11, p. 95).

[94] In one of the Notes to the Unknown Reader, that follows ("The Sidereal Eiffel Tower", Cendrars reports that J.D. Littlepage, "the American specialist who collaborated for ten years on the industrial equipment of Siberian gold mines" planted the seed of this news item in *A la recherche des mines d'or de Sibérie* (Payot, Paris, 1939) when he made the following comment: "We know that Stalin is a great readers of novels, just as we know that Churchill was a painter, probably to seek relief from affairs of state. He added: "The translation of *Gold* into Russian was made without my knowledge by Victor Serge and was published under the title of Zoloto, also without my knowledge, by the Editions d'Etat (?) Leningrad 1929" (TADA 12, p. 348).

[95] Confusion of Cendrars: Victor Serge did not translate *Gold* but prefaced the translation made by O. Brochnikovskaia and published in 1926, by Editions d'Etat, Moscow-Leningrad. During the same year, another translation of the novel by Mr Simonobtich was published by Editions Prométéi, Moscow. On V. Serge, see infra note 124.

[96] Al Jennings (1863-1961), Oklahoma attorney, became the leader of a gang specialized in train robberies in 1897. He was sentenced to five years imprisonment during which time he met the writer O Henry. Subsequently, he worked as Technical director in the movie business and became a writer himself. Cendrars translated his work « *Hors-la-loi! La vie d'un outlaw américain racontée par lui-même"* (Grasset, 1936) and the novella : « *Au Bidon de Sang* » that he reprinted in *Histoires vraies,* introducing it by the tale of their meeting in Hollywood (1937 ; TADA 8, p. 83-107).

[97] The two volumes of *"Têtes brûlées"* were published by Edtions du Sans Pareil in 1930 (Brignolf, no 1) and 1931 (Al Capone, no 2)

[98] "Le Saint inconnu" was published in *Histoires vraies* (1937; TADA 8, p. 67-81).

[99] Cendrars labeled Saint Joseph of Cupertino (1603-1663) "the new patron saint of aviation" in *Le Lotissement du Ciel* (1949. TADA 12; p. 21-181);

[100] Voltaire did not ridicule Saint Joseph of Cupertino but rather Saint Cucuron. Cendrars had already confused this in "Le Nouveau Patron de l'aviation" (TADA 12, p. 181, Note XLIV to the Unknown Reader).

[101] *Moravagine*, chapter p) Aviation (TADA 7, p. 188-196).

[102] This influence of Fantomas is emphasized by Cendrars in "Moravagine : Story of a book" (La Gazette des lettres, August 15, 1952) and would become "Pro domo/How I wrote Moravagine" in a new edition of the book released in 1956 (TADA 7, p. 228-229). See also note 118.

[103] Cendrars describes Antoine de Saint-Exupéry (1900-1944) in "Anecdotique", one of the novellas of *La Vie Dangereuse* (1938; TADA 8, p. 215-222). Consuelo Suncin (1901-1979), painter and sculptor orginally from El Salvador, married the writer in 1931.

[104] Charles-Ferdinand Ramuz (1878-1947), the most celebrated writer of French-speaking Switzerland, is the contrary of Cendrars who wanted to lead his life "on a global plan"; The relations between the two writers would appear to have been very sporadic. Another allusion to Ramuz appears in "Mes chasses" (D'Oultremer à Indigo, TADA 8, p. 349)

INTERVIEW VIII

Interview VIII is a reworked version of the sixth radio interview.

[105] On armadillo hunting, see *L'Homme Foudroyé* (TADA 5, p. 335)

[106] The last section of Kodak is presented as a list of "Menus" (TADA 1, p. 174-175)

[107] Jean Voilier is the pseudonym of Jeanne Loviton (1903-1996). After practicing law in the firm of Maurice Garçon, she married the novelist Pierre Frondaie and became a woman of influence, notorious for her beauty, her ambition and more discreetly for multiple liaisons, notably with Jean Giraudoux and Saint-John Perse. Under her pen name, she published three novels. From 1937 on, she was the great secret love of Paul Valéry when she met Robert Denoel in December 1942. In May, 1945, she revealed this new liaison to the poet who did not survive the confession. Coming from Liège to Paris in 1926, Denoel (1902-1945) went into publishing and triumphed in 1932 with Céline, his fetish author's, *Journey to the End of the Night*. Denoel published Céline's pamphlets and maintained very difficult relations. At the outset of the war, the man nicknamed the "Belgian Rastignac" became a premier rank publisher with a rich catalogue (Aragon, Tzara, Artaud, Elsa Triolet…) Continuing to ply his trade during the occupation, he published both Elsa Triolet and Lucien Rebatet. In the wake of the Liberation, he was accused of collaboration and prepared his defense with Jeanne Loviton. On the day prior to his trial, on December 2, 1945, Robert Denoel was murdered on the Boulevard des Invalides, nearby his vehicle. Was he fixing a flat tire, or was he the victim of a political-financial ambush? The conduct of Jeanne Loviton who accompanied him that day was the subject of contradictory statements but the circumstances of the crime were never officially investigated. At the time of the settling of the estate, a dispute broke out between the publisher's wife, Cécile, whom he was in the process of divorcing, and his companion, who possessed a *blanc seing* (power of attorney) on Robert Denoel's shares. After a long trial (1946-1950), Jean Voilier prevailed in the lawsuit. In 1951, she sold Editions Denoel to Gaston Gallimard. Louise Staman shed some brutal light on the fascinating and ambiguous person-

ality of Jeanne Loviton-Jean Voilier and the background of this nebulous affair in *Assassinat d'un éditeur à la Libération. Robert Denoel (1902-1945)* (Paris, èditeur, 2005).

[108] This is the dedication to the "*Première Rhapsodie Gitane*" (*L'Homme Foudroyé*, TADA 5, p. 169). Rosita Guzman (1879-1976) became the Viscountess Jean de Contades, and the Countess François de Castries. Of Mexican origin, she was very close to Eugenia Errazurriz, the Chilien friend of Cendrars and to Abbot Mugnier (« the blind Abbot ») – she was one of his two nieces, with Princess Bibesco. This worldly Abbot bequeathed her his Journal, where she is often referred to. She was a very intimate friend of Cendrars and the principal model for the character of Paquita.

[109] In the end, he did not compose it.

[110] While manning a petrol station "in the depths of the immensities of Brazil", Manolo Secca carved out 308 characters from wood that he composed as the twelve [SIC] stations of the Cross (*L'Homme Foudroyé*, TADA 5, p. 337-339). In this character, Cendrars transposed the figure of Antonio Francisco Lisboa, aka Aleijadinho, "the little cripple", Brazilian baroque sculptor and architect with the mutilated hands (1738-1814), with whom he planned on writing a book. Aleijadinho is famous for the churches that he constructed in Ouro Preto (Minas Gerais) and for the Congonhas sanctuary, his masterpiece that contained a stations of the cross that Cendrars proposes here as a burlesque version.

[111] Oswaldo Padroso is the melancholic hero of "The Sidereal Eiffel Tower" (*Sky*, TADA 12,). Hopelessly in love with Sarah Bernhardt, this Brazilian *fazendeioro* rancher lived reclusively on his property in Morro Azul. His adventure is a mirror reflection of Cendrars relationship with Raymone.

[112] During the filming of *la Voyante*, Sarah Bernhardt, seventy-nine years old, died of exhaustion on March 26, 1923. She had requested that this Franco-American production of *Films Abdures*, directed by a Frenchman (and not an American), Louis Mercanton, be filmed at her residence.

[113] Cendrars travelled to Hollywood at the instigation of his friend Pierre Lazareff. His reportage "Hollywood 1936" was published in *Paris-soir* from May 31 to June 13, 1936. At the end of the same year, this reportage was published in a volume by Grasset, under the title, *Hollywood, the*

Mecca of Cinema, with 29 drawings of Jean Guérin (TADA 3, p. 1-137).

[114] Cendrars admired Walt Disney (1901-1966) whom he considered to be an "assembly-line poet". When he travelled on a journalistic mission to Hollywood in 1936, he did not succeed in meeting the director who had since become an independent producer. Mickey Mouse was baptized and soundtracked in 1928. Donald, Pluto and Goofy followed in succession. *Three Little Pigs* (1933) made Disney a fortune, and he commercially exploited his creations (books, records, miscellaneous toys). In 1937, he produced *Snow White and the Seven Dwarfs*.

INTERVIEW IX

Interview IX is a reworked version of the seventh radio interview

[115] Ernest Hemingway (1896-1961) spoke of his sole meeting with Cendrars in mixed terms: "He was a good companion until he drank too much, and at that time, when he was lying, he was more interesting than many men telling a story truly." And, in a more cruel aside, he added that "Cendrars could have been a bit more discreet on the loss of his arm (*A Moveable Feast*, 1964; Folio, p. 98-99).

[116] During late January 1930, Cendrars met the American writer John Dos Passos (1896-1970) in Monpazier. During the previous Autumn, he had learned in Paris about the man who qualified him as the "Homer of the Transsiberian" in Orient Express (1927; Editions du Rocher, 1991, p. 253-274). Dos Passos had already started translating Cendrar's poems into English. He published them upon his return to the United States, also inserting watercolours. This rare volume is reproduced in fac-similé in *Voyager avec Blaise Cendrars* (La Quinzaine littéraire-Louis Vuitton, 1994).

[117] "*L'Affaire Galmot*" was published in serial form in the October 8- to December 17, 1930, and was later compiled into one volume under the title *Rhum* (Grasset 1930; TADA 2, p. 155-299). This was Cendrars' first reportage. His career as a journalist began developing in 1934 (TADA 13).

[118] Cendrars first crossed paths with Henry Miller (1891-1980) between December 14-18, 1934 at 18 Villa Seurat (Paris 14ième) where the Amer-

ican writer was residing. Notable encounter: On January 1, 1935, Cendrars published his review of *Tropic of Cancer* in the review *Orbes*, which constitutes the first article published in France on Miller (TADA 11, p. 136-137). In *Blaise Cendrars* (Denoel, 1951) and *The Books of my Life* (trad. Gallimard, 1957), Miller expressed deep admiration for Cendrars, whereas the latter meted out his praise in smaller doses in their correspondence (Denoel, 1995). On H. Miller, see F.J. Temple who was a friend of the two writers, *Henry Miller* (1965; Buchet-Chastel, 2004).

[119] Moran viewed William Seabrook (1886-1945) as an American Cendrars. This journalist and writer attained international renown with *The Magic Island* (1929) a reportage on Haiti and voodoo. Cendrars refers to it in *Rhum* (TADA 2 p. 281-282) and in *Bourlinguer* (TADA 9, 206).

[120] Freddy Sauser enjoyed giving the barman his former first name.

[121] Indeed.

[122] Cendrars delivered *Rimsky-Korsakov et les maîtres de la musique russe* to Editions Eugène Figuière in December 1912, and corrected the proofs in February 1913. But the volume was never published and the text was only finally published in August 1919 in *La Renaissance politique, littéraire, économique* (nos 17 and 18) republished under the title: "*Rimsky-Korskov et ses aînés*" in Le Nouvel Âge in April 1931. Miriam Cendrars republished it as a supplement to her edition of *Aujourd'hui* (Denoel, 1987), p. 207-234).

[123] Replaces Petrouchka in the personal copy of Cendrars.

[124] The script of *Après-diner, ballet* was published by Miriam Cendrars who retraced the misadventures in "*Les métamorphoses parisiennes d'un ballet suédois*" (Continent Cendrars, no 1, Neuchâtel, A la Baconnière, 1986, p. 12-23).

[125] The long, highly chequered career of Marguerite Moreno (1871-1948), née Marguerite Monceau, led this famous actress of the Comédie-Françàise to the cabarets and from Racine to the cinema where she held a role as an undignified old biddy in numerous B-movies. When he returned from American after the Second World War. Louis Jouvet offered him the role of her life, with the character of Aurélie, the Folle de Chaillot, in the homonymous play by Jean Giraudoux. The success of this play, created on December 22, 1945 at the Théâtre de l'Athénée, was considerable

and is inseparable from that of its lead actress. The show was finally closed due to exhaustion of the actors. Raymone was also part of the cast, playing the role of Gabrielle, the Folle de Saint-Sulpice. Numerous elements – age, loquaciousness, career and personal life – would indicate that Marguerite Moreno is the model for Thérèse Eglantine, the truculent heroine of *Emmènes-moi au bout du monde!*…(1956; TADA 14).

[126] Ricciotto Canudo (1879-1923), an Italian writer residing in France, signed with Cendrars a "Call" published in the print press on July 29, 1914, inviting ex-patriot friends of France to enlist. Canudo directed the review Montjoie!, "organ of French artistic Imperialism" (1913-1914), and Cendrars was a contributor. He invented the expression 7th art to designate cinema. Cendrars refers to him in "Mardi Gras", the 8th of the *Nineteen elastic poems* (1919 TADA 1, p. 78) and recalled his novel *Les Transplantés* (1913), when he wrote *Moravagine*. Canudo introduced Raymone to Cendrars on October 26, 1917.

[127] This was a scene based on dialogue of Cendrars at the front with this amateur investigator of modern poetry (*La Main Coupée*, 1946; TADA 6, p. 252-253).

[128] Erik Satie (1866-1925) was the "patron" of the *Lyre et Palette* evenings held in the salle Huyghens, Montparnasse in 1917. Painters, musicians and poets met in the studio of the Swiss sculptor Emile Lejeune at the initiative of Cendrars. Reoriented – or hijacked – by Cocteau, these meetings engendered the foundation of the Group of Six in 1920. Satie, who served as spiritual elder to this group, despite not being a member, consciously cultivated his legend as an excentric musician, notably by the incognuous titles he gave to his works. Cendrars considered his music as one of the seven wonders of the modern world because you could actually listen to it "without burying your head in your hands" (*Aujourd'hui*; TADA 11, p. 118.

INTERVIEW X

Most of this final interview is absent from the radio interview, particularly the burial of Apollinaire. Whether it disappeared with the excising of the first scene is a matter of conjecture, but it appears doubtful. In a later show of André Gillois, "*Soyez témoins*", broadcast on April 6, 1956, Cendrars enriched his written version of the burial with new details: the presence at the side of Jacqueline Apollinaire of Eugenia Errazurriz or the placing under seal of Apollinaire's apartment due to the intervention of his mother.

[129] Notwithstanding this denial, Cendrars elected to conclude *Blaise Cendrars Speaks...* by a long narrative of the final days of Apollinaire and his burial. Although the accuracy of the facts that he reports is scarcely confirmed by the biographers of "poor Guillaume" this "tragic calendar" proposes a sort of tomb of Apollinaire. Cendrars buries his friend a second time, rendering a homage that is remarkably ambiguous.

[130] After an initial version published in 1904 in the review *Le Festin d'Esope*, The Rotting Wizard – who was Merlin – was published with Henry Kahnweiler in 1909, with monochromatic woodcuts contributed by André Derian. Long ignored by the critics, this unclassifiable text which combines elements of tales, poems and theatre is considered today as a major work (Apollinaire, *Oeuvres en prose*, I, Ed; Michel Décaudin, 1977, p. 5-80; notes, p. 1065-1107). A critical edition was procured by Jean Burgos in a Minard *Lettres Modernes* edition in 1972.

[131] Better known under the pseudonym of Serge Férat, the Count Edouard Serge Jastrebzoff (1881-1958), Russian painter, was the creator of the décor, stage and costumes of the *Mamelles de Tirésias*. With his foster sister Hélène d'OEttingen, he funded the second series of the *Soirées de Paris* (1913-1914). During the Great War, he was a nurse at the hospital of the Italian Government in Paris, where he had Apollinaire admitted after he was wounded.

[132] Pierre Albert-Birot (1876-1967), poet, novelist and playright, directed the review *Sic* (1916-1919). He organized the production of the Mamelles de Tirésias.

[33] The collaboration of Apollinaire with the *Bibliothèque des Curieux* began in 1908. Funded by the Briffaut brothers, this publishing house was established on the rue de Furstenberg. in five years, Apollinaire edited fourteen volumes in the collection "*Les Maîtres de l'amour*" and a similar number in the "*Coffret du bibliophile*" collection, and both enjoyed wide public acclaim. He planned on rapidly merging his prefaces and notices into one volume, but although the manuscript was deposited in 1914 with

Mercure de France under the title *Les Diables amoureux*, the volume was only published in 1964 by Gallimard. On these adventures, see the edition produced by Mr Décaudin for Tome III of Apollinaire's *Oeuvres en prose complètes* in the "Bibliothèque de la Pléiade" (Gallimard, 1993).

[134] Emile Jules Grillot de Givry (1874-1929) cabalist and occultist admired by J.-K Huysmans, translated Paracelsus. Among his books are *Le Grand Oeuvre* (1907) and *Le Musée des sorciers, mages et alchimistes* (1929). *L'Anthologie de l'occultisme. Choix des meilleures pages des auteurs qui se sont illustrés dans les sciences hermétiques depuis les temps anciens jusqu'à nos jours* constitutes the 4th volume of the « Collection des Anthologies » published by Cendrars at la Sirène. Grillot de Givry is credited with translations, notices and preface, butthe true author according to Cendrars, who nevertheless doesn't disclose the name, is Conrad Moricand (1887-1954), the Swiss astrologist. The poet apparently met him during the Great War and their friendship appears to have ben close until their rupture in the thirties. He published Moricand's *Les Interprètes* at La Sirène (1919) and dedicated "Académie Médrano", one of the Sonnets dénaturés to him (written in November 1916; TADA 1, p. 112) and The Druid, jointly to Jacques Doucet (TADA 7, p. 287 and p. 372). Moricand drew the "unique hand" of his friend for the frontispice of Aujourd'hui (TADA 11, p. xxxii) and a portrait allegedly of Moravagine (TADA 7, p. 222). Cendrars attributes to Moricand the astrological portrait of Jean Galmot inserted in *Rhum* (TADA 2, p. 167-169). For Henry Miller, who hosted him in 1947 in Big Sur (California), he wrote: "he was an incurable dandy leading the life of a tramp" (*A devil in paradise*, 1957). It is perhaps due to the influence of Moricand that Cendrars picked up his esoteric culture, that Abel Gance testified was vast (Mercure de France, special number on Cendrars, 1962, p. 170).

[135] Joseph-Charles Mardrus (1868-1949), Egyptian, was a doctor passionate for travel and orientalism. Encouraged by Mallarmé, he translated, according to Galland, *The Thousand and One Nights*, from 1898-1904. He was an influential actor on the Parisian stage. The novelist Lucie Delarue-Mardrus was his first spouse.

[136] In fact, Apollinaire deleted the punctuation and replaced Eau-de-Vie by Alcools in the first proofs of the collection during late October 1912. Was it at the suggestion of Cendrars? The book was published in Mercure de France with an imprint date of April 20, 1913.

[137] Confusion on dates: It was the previous year, in 1910, that L'Hérésiarque et Cie obtained votes for the Goncourt prize, eventually awarded for another collection of tales, De Goupil à Margot, by Louis Pergaud.

[138] Poet, typographer and printer, François Bernouard (1884-1948) set up his studio at 71 rue des Saints-Pères (Sixth arrondissement), the building where Rémy de Gourmont lived, the writer admired by Cendrars. Is it through him that the poet became acquainted with the publisher? Bernouard published two deluxe plaquettes (booklets) of Cendrars that have endured: Profond aujourd'hui, with five illustrations by Angel Zarraga (1917), and J'ai Tué (I have killed), with five illustrations by Fernand Léger (1918). In 1931, these plaquetttes were brought together in Aujourd'hui without the illustrations (the TADA 11 version reinserts them, p. 2-16). Bernouard published books under four trade names: his patronym, la Typographie de François Bernouard, A Schéhérazade and A la Belle Edition which he founded in 1909 with Louis Jou, another prominent typographer. Attentive to trends, Bernouard published deluxe books under a cover illustrated by a red rose drawn by Paul Iribe. Specializing in books on painters, Bernouard launched into the publication of Complete Works editions during the nineteen-twenties (Nerval, Mérimée, Barbey, Zola, Schwob...) that he rarely managed to bring to fruition. A Catalogue des impressions de feu Monsieur Bernouard was written by G.A. Dassonville (Bagnolet, La Typographie, 1988).

[139] It's probably this tube of Harlem oil that is referred to discreetly by the expression « Beau cheval écumant » that appears in Le Panama (TADA 1, p. 58) and in Profond Aujourd'hui (TADA 11, p. 8).

[140] Pico Pere Pedro Creixams (1893-1965), Catalan painter, arrived in Paris in 1918, where François Bernourard hired him as a typographer. He was known as a painter of Montmartre Bohemia and of scenes of Spanish life.

[141] Albert Gervais Capmas (1873-1958), friend of Paul Laffitte, was the physician at La Sirène. Pascal Fouché reports that after completing his studies in medicine at Lyon, he became a doctor for the Legion: "Seriously injured in the war he arrived in Paris at 7, rue Saint Philippe-du-Roule in 1918. He attended at Apollinaire's deathbed, and that of Radiguet five years later. He was also the physician of Cocteau and of Gance" (La Sirène, Bibliothèque de Littérature française contemporaine de l'université Paris 7, 1984, p. 294).

[142] "Wednesday 13" replaces "Monday 11" in the personal copy of Cendrars.

[143] Through Paul Laffitte, the proprietor of Editions de la Sirène, Cendrars met Abel Gance (1889-1981) who was looking for survivors of the Great War for certain scenes in *J'accuse*. Filming started in the Nice studios in August 1918, the film was released in March 1919. As assistant director, Cendrars also made a cameo appearance in the famous scene of the dead who rise up on the battle field to accuse the living. He then had a role as "director" (Gance dixit) during the shooting of *La Roue* between Nice, Arcachon, Saint-Gervais and Mont Blanc. During the shoot, he also worked on his novel *Dan Yack* ("*le Plan de l'Aiguille*") that he dedicated to Gance in 1929 (TADA 4, see in the file, notes 2, 78, 98 and 116). Gance described their friendship and his admiration for the poet in Prisme (Gallimard, 1930). He was much more reserved in his praise where it concerned his talents in the field of movie production (Mercure de France, special Cendrars issue, 1962, p. 170-171).

[144] More precisely, between October 15 and November 30, 1950.

[145] Poet, journalist, and radio man, Paul Gilson (1904-1963) was the Director of Artistic Services at RTF from 1946 up until his death. Under the general direction of Wladimir Porché, he played an eminent role. Multiplying the rebroadcasting of shows and programmes produced in-studio, he assigned a "Poetry Office" to André Beucler and programmes to other poets (Philippe Soupault, Loys Masson, Georges-Emmanuel Clancier). With Henri Barraud, he favoured contemporary music and created the first weekly radio magazine on the plastic arts ("Art and life" in 1946, and then "How to look at painting" with René Huyghe). He was also behind the "*Petit conservatoire de la chanson*" of Mireille. He was a great friend of Cendrars whom he knew during the pre-war days at Radio-Luxembourg. In his programme "*Banc d'essai*", he broadcast adaptations of *Du monde entier* (1938). *L'Opéra inachevé* (1939) and *Gold* (1939). After the war, he frequently invited Cendrars as a guest on RTF, particularly for these interviews with Michel Manoll (1950) and for the three *Films sans images*. During the same year, he invited Cendrars to spend several weeks at his castle in La Marche, nearby La Charité-sur-Loire (Nièvre) at the time Cendrars was working on his "novel-novel", *Emmène-moi au bout du monde*…which in 1956 would be dedicated "to the grand Paul", an affectionate and admiring nickname that friends gave to Gilson. *Trop c'est trop, "Nuit à New York"* is also dedicated to Paul and to Christiane Gilson

(TADA 11, p. 353-355). Poet, (Poems 1950; Enigmarelle, 1963), attentive to a broad range of demonstrations of the unusual (Merveilleux, 1945), Paul Gilson was the testamentary executor of Cendrars whom he survived for only a short time.

About Blaise Cendrars

Frédéric-Louis Sauser (September 1, 1887 – January 21, 1961), better known as Blaise Cendrars, was a Swiss-born novelist and poet who became a naturalized French citizen in 1916. He was a writer of considerable influence in the European modernist movement. He was born in La Chaux-de-Fonds, Neuchâtel, Switzerland, rue de la Paix 27, to a bourgeois francophone family. They sent young Frédéric to a German boarding school, but he ran away. At the Realschule in Basel in 1902 he met his lifelong friend the sculptor August Suter. Next they enrolled him in a school in Neuchâtel, but he had little enthusiasm for his studies. Finally, in 1904, he left school due to poor performance and began an apprenticeship with a Swiss watchmaker in Russia.

In 1907, Sauser returned to Switzerland, where he studied medicine at the University of Berne. During this period, he wrote his first verified poems, Séquences, influenced by Remy de Gourmont's Le Latin mystique.

Cendrars was the first exponent of Modernism in European poetry with his works: *The Legend of Novgorode* (1907), *Les Pâques à New York* (1912), *La Prose du Transsibérien et la Petite Jehanne de France* (1913), *Séquences* (1913), *La Guerre au Luxembourg* (1916), *Le Panama ou les aventures de mes sept oncles* (1918), *J'ai tué* (1918), and *Dix-neuf poèmes élastiques* (1919). He was the first modernist poet, not only in terms of expressing the fundamental values of Modernism but also in terms of creating its first solid poetical synthesis, although this achievement did not grow out of a literary project or any theoretical considerations but from Cendrars' instinctive attraction to all that was new in the age and equally alive for him in literature of the past.

In many ways, he was a direct heir of Rimbaud, a visionary rather than what the French call un homme de lettres ("a man of letters"), a term that for him was predicated on a separation of intellect and life. Like Rimbaud, who writes in "The Alchemy of the Word" in *A Season in Hell*, "I liked absurd paintings over door panels, stage sets, backdrops for acrobats, signs, popular engravings, old-fashioned literature, church Latin, erotic books full of misspellings," Cendrars similarly says of himself in *Der Sturm* (1913), "I like legends, dialects, mistakes of language, detective novels, the flesh of girls, the sun, the Eiffel Tower."

Spontaneity, boundless curiosity, a craving for travel, and immersion in actualities were his hallmarks both in life and art. He was drawn to this same immersion in Balzac's flood of novels on 19th-century French society and in Casanova's travels and adventures through 18th-century Europe, which he set down in dozens of volumes of memoirs that Cendrars considered "the true Encyclopedia of the eighteenth century, filled with life as they are, unlike Diderot's, and the work of a single man, who was neither an ideologue nor a theoretician." Cendrars regarded the early modernist movement from roughly 1910 to the mid-1920s as a period of genuine discovery in the arts and in 1919 contrasted "theoretical cubism" with "the group's three antitheoreticians," Picasso, Braque, and Léger, whom he described as "three strongly personal painters who represent the three successive phases of cubism."

After a short stay in Paris, he traveled to New York, arriving on 11 December 1911. Between 6–8 April 1912, he wrote his long poem, *Les Pâques à New York* (*Easter in New York*), his first important contribution to modern literature. He signed it for the first time with the name Blaise Cendrars.

In the summer of 1912, Cendrars returned to Paris, convinced that poetry was his vocation. With Emil Szittya, an anarchist writer, he started the journal Les hommes nouveaux, also the name of the press where he published Les Pâques à New York and Séquences. He became acquainted with the international array of artists and writers in Paris, such as Chagall, Léger, Survage, Suter, Modigliani, Csaky, Archipenko, Jean Hugo and Robert Delaunay.

Most notably, he encountered Guillaume Apollinaire. The two poets influenced each other's work. Cendrars' poem "Les Pâques à New York" influenced Apollinaire's poem "Zone." Cendrars' style was based on photographic impressions, cinematic effects of montage and rapid changes of imagery, and scenes of great emotional force, often with the power of a hallucination. These qualities, which also inform his prose, are already evident in *Easter in New York* and in his best known and even longer poem *The Transsiberian*, with its scenes of revolution and the Far East in flames in the Russo-Japanese war ("The earth stretches elongated and snaps back like an accordion / tortured by a sadic hand / In the rips in the sky insane locomotives / Take flight / In the gaps / Whirling wheels mouths voices / And the dogs of disaster howling at our heels"). The published work was printed within washes of color by the painter Sonia Delaunay-Terk as a fold-out two meters in length, together with her design of brilliant colors down the left-hand side, a small map of the Transsiberian railway in the upper right corner, and a painted silhouette in orange of the Eiffel Tower in the lower left. Cendrars called the work first "simultaneous poem". Soon after, it was exhibited as a work of art in its own right and continues to be shown at exhibitions to this day.

His writing career was interrupted by World War I. When it began, he and the Italian writer Ricciotto Canudo appealed to other foreign artists to join the French army. He joined the French Foreign Legion. He was sent to the front line in the Somme where from mid-December 1914 until February 1915, he was in the line at Frise (La Grenouillère and Bois de la Vache). He described this war experience in the books *La Main coupée* (*The severed hand*) and *J'ai tué* (*I have killed*), and it is the subject of his poem "Orion" in Travel Notes: "It is my star / It is in the shape of a hand / It is my hand gone up to the sky . . ." It was during the attacks in Champagne in September 1915 that Cendrars lost his right arm and was discharged from the army.

Cendrars became an important part of the artistic community in Montparnasse; his writings were considered a literary epic of the modern adventurer. He was a friend of the American writer Henry Miller, who called him his "great idol," a man he "really venerated as a writer." He knew many of the writers, painters, and sculptors living in Paris. In 1918, his friend Amedeo Modigliani painted his portrait. He was acquainted with Ernest Hemingway, who mentions having seen him "with his broken boxer's nose and his pinned-up empty sleeve, rolling a cigarette with his one good hand," at the Closerie des Lilas in Paris. He was also befriended by John

Dos Passos, who was his closest American counterpart both as a world traveler (even more than Hemingway) and in his adaptation of Cendrars' cinematic uses of montage in writing, most notably in his great trilogy of the 1930s, *U.S.A.* One of the most gifted observers of the times, Dos Passos brought Cendrars to American readers in the 1920s and 30s by translating Cendrars' major long poems *The Transsiberian* and *Panama* and in his 1926 prose-poetic essay "Homer of the Transsiberian," which was reprinted from *The Saturday Review* one year later in *Orient Express*.

After the war, Cendrars became involved in the movie industry in Italy, France, and the United States. Cendrars' departure from poetry in the 1920s roughly coincided with his break from the world of the French intellectuals, summed up in his *Farewell to Painters* (1926) and the last section of *L'homme foudroyé* (1944), after which he began to make numerous trips to South America ("while others were going to Moscow," as he writes in that chapter). It was during this second half of his career that he began to concentrate on novels, short stories, and, near the end and just after World War II, on his magnificent poetic-autobiographical tetralogy, beginning with *L'homme foudroyé.*

Cendrars continued to be active in the Paris artistic community, encouraging younger artists and writing about them. For instance, he described the Hungarian photographer Ervin Marton as an "ace of white and black photography" in a preface to his exhibition catalogue. He was with the British Expeditionary Force in northern France at the beginning of the German invasion in 1940, and his book that immediately followed, *Chez l'armée anglaise* (*With the English Army*), was seized before publication by the Gestapo, which sought him out and sacked his library in his country home, while he fled into hiding in Aix-en-Provence. He comments on the trampling of his library and temporary "extinction of my personality" at the beginning of *L'homme foudroyé* (in the double sense of "the man who was blown away"). In Occupied France, the Gestapo listed Cendrars as a Jewish writer of "French expression," but he managed to survive. His youngest son was killed in an accident while escorting American planes in Morocco. Details of his time with the BEF and last meeting with his son appear in his work of 1949 *Le lotissement du ciel* (translated simply as *Sky*).

In 1950, Cendrars settled down in the rue Jean-Dolent in Paris, across from the La Santé Prison. There he collaborated frequently with Radiodiffusion Française. He finally published again in 1956. The novel, *Emmène-moi au bout du monde!...*, was his last work before he suffered a stroke in 1957. He died in 1961. His ashes are held at Le Tremblay-sur-Mauldre.

About the Editor

Jim Christy grew up in Philadelphia, led a knockabout life in the United States which included carnivals, hoboing, and professional boxing, was involved in radical politics and moved to Canada in 1968. As well as being a writer, he is also a widely exhibited visual artist and has recorded CDs of poetry and music and performed in various countries. His travels have taken him from the Yukon to the Amazon, Greenland to Cambodia. The author of more than thirty books, including poetry, short stories, novels, travel and biography, Christy has been praised by writers as diverse as Charles Bukowski and Sparkle Hayter. Recent publications include the poetry book *The Big Thirst* (Ekstasis Editions, 2014) and the nonfiction book *Rogues, Rascals, and Scalawags Too* (Anvil Press, 2015).

About the Translator

David MacKinnon is a Vancouver, Canada-born novelist. After reading history and philosophy at the universities of British Columbia and Louvain (Belgium), and at Université de Paris IV-Sorbonne (Paris), he worked in the Alberta oilfields and at a series of jobs on the assembly line prior to being admitted to the Montreal bar, where he practiced as a trial lawyer. In '89, MacKinnon left for Hong Kong to assist Chinese nationals to escape the crackdown which followed the Tiananmen Square uprising and narrowly escaped himself after a group of Shanghai busninessmen attempted to coerce him into a people-smuggling scheme. In 2004, during an extended sojourn in the Seychelles, he was declared *persona non grata* for writing on the money and gun laundering engaged in by the tinpot dictatorship which runs the Seychelles to this day. David MacKinnon has written eight novels, including *Leper Tango* and *The Eel* (Guernica Editions).